KALKI GITA

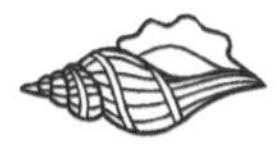

KALKI GITA

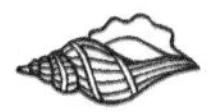

CHYREN SELIN

ZORBA BOOKS

ZORBA BOOKS

Published by Zorba Books, April 2023
Website: www.zorbabooks.com
Email: info@zorbabooks.com

Title: **Kalki Gita**

Author Name: Chyren Selin

Copyright © Chyren Selin

Printbook ISBN :- 978-93-95217-59-0

Ebook ISBN :- 978-93-95217-58-3

The publisher under the guidance and direction of the author has published the contents in this book, and the publisher takes no responsibility for the contents, its accuracy, completeness, any inconsistencies, or the statements made. The contents of the book do not reflect the opinion of the publisher or the editor. The publisher and editor shall not be liable for any errors, omissions, or the reliability of the contents of the book.

Any perceived slight against any person/s, place or organization is purely unintentional.

Zorba Books Pvt. Ltd. (opc)
Sushant Arcade,
Next to Courtyard Marriot,
Sushant Lok 1, Gurgaon – 122009, India

Printed by Manipal Technologies Limited
A1 & A2 Shivalli Industrial Area Manipal Udupi, Karnataka – 576104

CONTENTS

PREFACE

Vedanta is the heart and soul of Sanatan dharma, and as long as there will be debates, differences, and misunderstandings between the two schools of philosophy, that is, *dvait* and *advait*, the soul of Sanatan dharma won't be able to integrate itself and rise up to its full potential.

Therefore, I'm writing this book to end the long-going discussion between the two philosophies of Vedanta (advait and dvait) and clearing all the misunderstandings and loopholes that were being misunderstood by our traditional gurus only to distract people from the ultimate truth, were creating unnecessary divisions within Sanatan dharma, and were making it impossible for it to grow as one single united community. The ideas of extremist philosophies of both advait and dvait vedanta might actually be a conspiracy to divide and disintegrate Sanatan dharma, just like it was used earlier by the British against Indians to divide and conquer. That is why these must be rejected in order to save our Sanatan dharma. This is the time for the spiritual sun of Sanatana to rise again to its fullest of glory, and therefore, everyone must come together leaving behind all the misunderstandings and differences to meet at one point, i.e. the conclusion.

Most of the modern age spiritual gurus are misleading people with their half knowledge and have become spiritual dictators. All of their empires and followers are also built on the same old formula of British, which was to divide and rule, but it is only because they are incapable of comprehending the ultimate truth or the conclusion from the scriptures. The ultimate truth will never divide but only unify and integrate everything by bringing all of us together on an equal platform, which is why this book aims at re-integrating the ancient knowledge and wisdom of Sanatan and delivering the final conclusion. Those who will read and understand this Supreme knowledge will receive special grace from the Supreme Lord, and by spreading these words of ultimate wisdom, our Sanatan dharma will once again become flawless and shine in its fullest glory. The true purpose of Sanatan dharma is to create eternal immortal beings, or we can say that it is a dharma through which we can awaken our divinity and realise our original eternal Godly nature. However, due to certain confusions and to serve personal motives and dark agendas, the true knowledge of Santan dharma has been manipulated and was misunderstood since ages, which is causing it to deviate from its real purpose, that is, to produce eternal immortal and Godly beings that are eligible to live in the kingdom of the Supreme Lord.

Most people have become very materialistic, even though the spiritual knowledge and masters are easily available today. The reason being the materialistic model of the society is very well organised and structured, which is more reliable because the scientists agree on their material laws and principles, unlike the spiritual gurus today who keep on arguing on their concepts and never agreeing upon any one truth and coming to a decisive conclusion. As a result, unnecessary doubts and confusions arise in the minds of common people, making it almost impossible for them to accomplish their spiritual pursuits. Therefore, to replace this materialistic model of Kaliyuga with the spiritual model of Satyuga, the first challenge in front of us is to organise well the spiritual system or sector, which can only happen by delivering the ultimate spiritual knowledge that is based on facts from the scriptures as well as the practical experiences of our spiritual masters. This book aims at giving a kind of spiritual knowledge that is so well organised and structured, almost like our material science today, that it leaves no room for any doubts or arguments whatsoever, because we need to develop a kind of spiritual model so reliable that all kinds of people—logical, rational, or orthodox—can easily understand it first and then can easily believe in it because it will be based on the previously experienced states of our spiritual masters and eternal facts from our vedas and scriptures. The ultimate task in front of me was to come up with a decisive conclusion that is so simple to understand that even a child can easily learn from it and also believe in it just like science without any doubts. Because it is, in fact, the science of the spirit that is intended to help us progress in our spiritual journey and evolve together as spiritual beings if we only trust and believe in our spiritual concepts and principles just as much as we do with our scientific facts and concepts. Just like today in our materialistic society, we grow and function peacefully together as one human community, similarly, in future we can also create a new peacefully functioning and growth-oriented spiritual model for our society that can evolve together as one spiritual community. With the help of material science we can only improve the quality of our lives, but to enjoy the beauty and understand the real meaning of life, we must harness the power of our spiritual science. To start the golden age of Satyuga, it is necessary for all humans to find the balance between our material and spiritual growth model because both of them are equally necessary and can't be neglected, especially at this point in time where the balance between both the worlds of matter and spirit has already been disturbed to such an extent that it is leading us very close towards our annihilation. The Kaliyuga model, when men use to derive their sense of strength by looking and fighting with enemies outside of themselves, has caused a lot of destruction and unnecessary wars in this world. That's why, in the future, to establish a peaceful and prosperous society for mankind, all men will need to evolve, and instead of looking for enemies outside of them, he will look inside and defeat all the weaknesses that stop him from becoming invincible. That is how the future men in the Satyuga model will find their real inner strength. And the best part is that, in the previous model of Kaliyuga, there could exist only one Samraat (king), but in the future model of Satyuga, I see a possibility for all men to become a true king of their own kind. Therefore, to save this world from the destructions of an apocalypse and start a golden age, this generation must restore the long lost balance between the two worlds of matter and spirit to save humanity from a grave disaster by the re-establishment of our original Sanatan dharma and igniting the fire of a great spiritual revolution within every heart that beats on this planet.

INTRODUCTION

Prophecies of Kabir:

Around 600 years ago, Kabir sahib fixed the date on which a messiah will descend to bring the Golden Age on earth.

Kabirji said that when 5500 years of Kaliyug would pass, a great Saint will descend on the earth, and that would be the beginning of a new era—the Golden age. At that time, people from all religion will get satnam (the true method of worship) from that Saint and attain Supreme peaceful place—Satyalok (Golok).

In the Golden Age, there would be peace and prosperity on earth because the messiah will put a stop to all the evils and wars. Everyone will leave evil habits and take shelter of the Supreme God through that great Saint. There would be no atrocity on earth, no hatred, no conflicts between countries, no boundaries, and no wars for a thousand years to come. All people will be virtuous and would worship the supreme God.

Prophecies of Nostradamus:

Michael de Nostradamus, a famous French astrologer and seer, while describing the identity of the great Chyren Selin, said that:

1. The Chyren Selin will appear in Asia in the land surrounded by three oceans, i.e. India.
2. He will neither be a Christian nor a Muslim, he will certainly be a follower of Sanatan dharma.
3. The mother of the Chyren Selin would have three sisters and that he will have four children—two sons and two daughters.
4. His wisdom and powers will be unlimited, and the world will bow before him. He will be the most powerful spiritual leader who will bring the Golden Age not only in India but on the entire earth.

The great Chyren will be the chief of the world, loved, feared, and unchallenged even at the Death; his name and praise will reach beyond the skies, and he will be content to be known only as a Victor.

Decode: Nostradamus said that the great chyren will become the chief of the world. He will be loved as much as he would be feared, i.e. no one would ever dare to do any wrong under his reign. The name and praise of that great Saint will reach beyond the skies. Not only the humans on earth but even the gods in heaven would praise him.

Prophecies of Jeane Dixon:

The American foreteller said in her prophecies that the great soul has already taken birth in a rural family in India, and he will direct, control, and manage a great spiritual revolution.

Prophecies of Lady Florence:

Foretold that the great Saint from India with his spiritual thinking will be so revolutionary that its spark will turn into an inferno that will spread in every nook and corner of the globe and will eliminate the darkness from the world forever.

Prof. Chiro, Mr. Vegilatin, Andreson from America, Lady Boriska from Hungry, and many other Astrologers have made predictions about the great spiritual leader who will rise from India and bring the Golden Age in the world.

Prophecies of the Bible:

1. Out of this body in the presence of God.
2. Experiencing God in all his fullness and not just in thoughts.
3. Being reunited with those who have gone before us.
4. Leaving a world that has become grossly evil and unholy.
5. Pain and suffering will no longer exist.
6. God will wipe the tears away.
7. Worry will be behind us.
8. We will enter the divine rest promised to us.
9. We will know as we are known.
10. We will witness the beauty of God.

11. We will witness the beauty of heaven.
12. Evil will not exist.
13. We will experience everlasting peace.
14. We will be surrounded by like-minded people fully with the mind of God.
15. Everyone will be continuously prosperous.
16. Hate will not exist.
17. Unforgiveness will not exist.
18. Everything will be in a state of perfection.
19. Love will rule.
20. Satan and demonic powers will not exist.
21. Humans will become immortal, and death will not exist.
22. Humans raptured will never experience death.
23. We will meet angelic beings.
24. We will meet saints and characters of Bible we have read about.
25. God will be near us always.
26. We will see God enjoying his creation first-hand.
27. We will experience a world without stress.
28. We will see the creation in perfect state.
29. There will be no bullies or abuse or criminals or prisons.
30. The raptured will be forever the bride of Christ (God) to rule and reign with him forever.
31. There shall never be thirst or hunger.
32. Everything will be pure.
33. Lost children will be found.
34. No one will wear glasses, prosthetic legs or arms, hearing aids, etc.
35. There will be no fear of the unknown future.

36. You will see the lamb lay down with the lion: Animals will live together in peace.
37. You will be with the LAMB who is the LION.
38. There will be no language barriers.
39. We will experience the greatest party of all time—The marriage supper of the LAMB.
40. We will eat off the finest table of all time—The marriage supper of the LAMB.
41. We will see God in all his glory.
42. We will be made perfect without any flaw.
43. We will never get old again.
44. There shall never be bad weather or disasters.
45. We will witness new creations of God.
46. We will see the New Jerusalem.
47. We will live in our new mansions made for us by God.
48. We will hear God singing over us.
49. We will hear angels singing.
50. We will hear all of heaven glorifying God in song and worship.
51. We will understand things we could never understand before.
52. There will be no mental health problems, and no one will be inferior.
53. There will be no culture or colour barriers.
54. There will be no darkness, only light—the light of God.
55. The streets will be made of Gold; gold would be that common.
56. Jewels will be common.
57. There will be no gossip or negativity.

58. The beauty of earth is only a poor glimpse of the coming beauty of Heaven and the New Jerusalem.
59. Sadness and depression will be non-existent.
60. We will laugh with God.
61. We will experience new lovely fragrances, sounds, tastes, and colours.
62. Everything will be made new.
63. There will never be torment or torture, child abuse, violence or war.
64. God will maintain the peace.
65. There will be no obesity or eating disorders.
66. We will never run out of time.
67. No one will steal, cheat, or lie.
68. Families will not be broken, and hearts will not be broken.
69. The bride shall never again be under the rule of the antichrist (evil).
70. The bride shall never be forced to choose between the mark of the beast or death.
71. You will make new friends.
72. You will enjoy the company of God endlessly.
73. There will be no disease, pestilence, decay, or death.
74. There will be no institutions for sick, elderly, or children's hospital.
75. People will only think good thoughts continuously.
76. Everyone will be in a state of physical perfection.
77. We will know all details behind the stories of the Bible.
78. We will know about heaven and life in heaven.
79. We will have the Mind of Christ.
80. We will experience true joy.

81. There will be pleasure at the right hand of God for ever more.

82. We will see all of God's original creation that have long been extinct from earth.

83. We will be cherished by God for all eternity.

84. We will witness the new heaven and new earth created by God for us.

85. There will be no corrupt governments.

86. There will be no evil tyranny or terrorist.

87. Hope shall never be lost again.

88. There shall never be hell or the lake of fire or eternal damnation.

89. Everyone will feel accepted—there will be no outcast or downcast or castaways.

90. We will witness Christ (God) in full control of the environment we are in, apart from the influence of Satan and the demonic.

91. We will have access to all the words ever written for God about his beauty and glory.

92. We will know all about the life of Christ (God) on earth.

93. We will know all the good works of the saints done in the will of the Father.

94. God will reward us, even for a cup of water that we gave a child.

95. We will be able to hug and thank Christ in person for what he did for us on the cross.

96. We will be able to sit in God's lap and look into his eyes and exchange words of love.

97. We will know the Holy Spirit, and he will be with us forever.

98. We shall return with Christ to earth to see him vanquish evil and destroy the works of evil men after the great tribulation.

99. We will experience true holiness for the first time ever.

100. Henceforth, there is laid up for me a crown of righteousness which the lord, the righteous judge, shall give me on that day, and not to me alone, but onto all.

ADIPURUSH AND ADIPRAKRITI

- ❖ 'Krsna' is known as 'Adipurush', and he is the objective or manifested form of 'Paramanand' or 'Super Bliss', i.e. 'Chidanand'.
- ❖ 'Radha' is known as 'Adiprakriti', and she is the subjective or unmanifested form of super bliss, also referred to as 'Paramprem' or 'Super Love'.
- ❖ The 'Rasik Saints' act as agents or bridge that links Radha with Krishna or vice versa. Therefore, those who want to attain the super bliss of Krsna and the super love of Radha must take the shelter of 'Rasik Saints'.
- ❖ For now, let us note that the manifested form of reality is known as 'objective reality', which always revolves around its 'subjective reality', and the latter remains hidden or unmanifested.

Thus, we can understand 'Krsna', i.e. Super bliss, is the manifested object that always revolves around its unmanifested subject 'Radha', i.e. Super love.

In fact, as mentioned in our scriptures, one of the names of Lord Krsna is 'Madan Mohan', which means the one who attracts even the cupid, and Shreemati Radhika is known as 'Madan Mohan Mohini', meaning the one who attracts Krsna himself.

Now, one thing that we must all understand about the objective reality is that it invariably exists in 'duality' as manifested and unmanifested objects; in addition, it can take multiple or infinite number of different shapes or forms. However, one thing is certain that all these objects of super bliss (Krsna), whether manifested or unmanifested, will always revolve around its unmanifested subject of super bliss, i.e. super love (Radha).

Let us also understand this concept from the example of our solar system where there are only nine objects, i.e. the planets that revolve around one subject—the Sun.

Now, there can be other solar systems where there can be more than nine planets because along with 'duality', the other aspect of objective reality is 'uncertainty'. However, regardless of how many shapes or forms manifest in the objective reality, the subjective reality always exists in singularity that is unmoved and always remains still in its position just like the Sun.

After understanding this scientific concept of objective and subjective reality, we can come to the conclusion that all the 'jiva-atmas', or living entities, are nothing but the manifestations of 'Adipurush' (Super bliss) and contribute as different parts or fragments of this grand objective reality that is made of super bliss (Krsna). Therefore, all the *jiva-atmas* are simply like planets that revolve around their one subject, i.e. super bliss (Krsna). This also explains the reason why all *jiva-atmas*, whether consciously or unconsciously, are always trying their best to be happy or blissful all the time.

Just like it is natural for a child to adapt its parents' characteristics, similarly, all living entities (*jiva-atmas*) have inherited or adopted the quality of being blissful from their father 'Krsna' who is none other than 'Super bliss' himself. The definition of bliss may differ from person to person, which is our free will to decide, but the ultimate desire of every being is to be in a blissful state, and nobody ever wants to suffer or feel pain. It is because bliss is what we are all made of, and it is the fundamental source of our origin or existence. Therefore, it is natural for all beings to get drawn or attracted towards all kinds of blissful experiences in life. Lord Krsna is known as super bliss because he is the real or permanent bliss that we are all seeking; however, due to our ignorance or lack of knowledge, we try to look for bliss outside of Krsna, in the unreal or temporary, known as *Maya* (illusion). Everything that exists in this creation actually exists within Lord Krsna and therefore belongs to him alone. It is only when we start to think or believe that something exists outside of Lord Krsna that we get ourselves trapped in illusion (*maya*) and consequently suffer in life. To redeem our original blissful state, the Lord wants us to surrender, which simply means to accept the fact that we are nothing but merely tiny fragments of super bliss (Krsna), and we do not have any separate identity other than the Lord. By knowing and accepting our original relationship with Lord Krsna, who is Super bliss himself, our process of surrender becomes complete, and we automatically develop an attachment or connection with the Lord; thereafter, by genuinely and unconditionally loving and serving him, we can also remain in a state of everlasting bliss just like our father Lord Krsna.

All the actions of our father Krsna (Superbliss) revolve around our mother Radha (Super love). Similarly, all our actions also always ultimately revolve around someone or something that we love. It could be an idea, a person, or a material object; anything that we love becomes the source or centre of our inspiration that drives all our actions.

With the help of this knowledge, we can also understand a very complex spiritual concept in a very simple way. There are several doubts and misunderstandings among all the spiritual aspirants as to how God evaluates or judges our Karmas (actions), and more importantly, on what basis.

The answer is very simple—while evaluating or judging our karmas, the Lord (God) is not at all concerned with the objective aspects of our actions (any action that is performed has three aspects, i.e. why, what, and how), that is, *what* and *how* we did something is ignored, only *why* we did something really matters and is actually examined. It is because the *why* is the subject around which *what* and *how* are bound to revolve, which means we have free will to decide only the *why*, i.e. the subjective part of our actions, and the rest of it (*what* and *how*, i.e. the objective part of our actions) follows on its own because it is the law of nature. Moreover, as we have already learnt before that the nature of objective reality is uncertain and complex, it is better for the Lord (God) to leave it 'unjudged'.

However, the *why* part is significant as it is the subjective truth of our actions or karmas that will remain unchanged and unaffected, making it much more convenient for the Lord to evaluate our actions and draw judgment accordingly.

There are mainly four types of 'WHY' that dictate all our actions in this material world and produce different kinds of results, which are as follows:

1. All actions that are performed keeping the 'ego' as the subject or all ego-centric actions that are performed for our own pleasure will lead us to 'hell'. It does not matter how many crores of rupees were donated as charity and what was done with it; if it was inspired by the ego, then such a man or woman goes to 'hell' (demon world).

2. All actions that are performed keeping 'family' as the subject or all family-centric actions that are performed for the welfare of our own family will lead us back to earth (human world).

3. All actions that are performed keeping 'society' as the subject or all society-centric actions that are performed for the welfare of our society will take us to heaven (demigods world).

4. All actions that are performed keeping 'God' as the subject or all God-centric actions that are performed for the pleasure of god will take us into the spiritual realms, that is, the kingdom of Gods.

In Bhagwat Gita, the sloka (V 18.66), where the Lord says to Arjuna, 'SARV DHARMAN PARITYAJYA MAM EKAM SHARANAM VRAJA, AHAM TVAM SARV-PAPEBHYO MOKSHAYISHYAMI MA SHUCAH' means to keep 'God' as the subject or inspiration (the *why*) of all our actions. Then, the *what* or *how* of our actions will not matter at all, and the Lord (God) shall liberate us from all our sins, and the soul will ultimately attain 'Moksha' (Ultimate Freedom).

- In the Mahabharat war, Arjuna killed so many soldiers and even had to kill some of his own relatives, but he was saved from all the sinful effects of his actions. This was only because it was performed keeping the Lord (God) as the 'subject', which rendered those actions divine (sin free), even though committing murder is the gravest of sins.

- Shree Krishna or Adipurusha is the embodiment of 'YogaMaya-Sakti' in its totality, just like Kali Maa or Prakriti is the total embodiment of 'Maya-Sakti'.

- Shree Radhe or Adiprakriti is the embodiment of 'Param Brahm' in its totality, just like Lord Shiva or Purusha is the total embodiment of 'Brahm'.

- This is so because in the transcendental realms of Adipurush and Adiprakriti, a mysterious exchange of energies takes place between the Masculine and the Feminine.

  Therefore;

- Krishna or Adipurush = (Para Prakriti + Apara Prakriti).

This also means that in the transcendental realm, Lord Krsna or 'Adipurusha' becomes the object of enjoyment; therefore, we can say that he is the objective super bliss. And as we have discussed earlier that the objective reality always exists in duality, it can be said that Krsna shows the unlimited and dynamic aspect of super bliss that is always manifesting itself into an infinite number of different shapes and forms.

❖ Radha or Adiprakriti = (Param Purush + Purush)

It means that in the transcendental realm, Shree Radha or 'Adiprakriti' becomes the subject of enjoyment or the enjoyer of super bliss (Krsna); therefore, she is the subjective super bliss, also known as 'super love'. In addition, because she is the subjective reality, she has the stability and continuity (Ananyata), unlike Krishna who is always changing into different shapes or forms and is very restless in nature. Therefore, to relieve himself from this restlessness, Krishna (Super bliss) keeps on searching or longing for Radha (super love) as it is only when they are together that Krsna (superbliss) can regain his lost sense of stability and find continuity of his existence.

❖ In the transcendental realm, the main goal of Adipurush (super bliss) is to serve Adiprakriti (super love), just like a wife serves her husband by taking a seed from her man and developing it into a fully grown baby. Similarly, Krishna (Super bliss) takes the seeds of super love from Shree Radha (Adiprakriti) and plants it in his 'causal body' that is made up of pure-consciousness, i.e. Shiv–Shakti. Subsequently, the seed grows and reaches his 'Subtle body' that is made up of absolute- consciousness, i.e. Laxmi–Narayan (all *muktis* or moksha reside in the subtle body of Krishna; this will be discussed later on). Finally, the seed grows completely and is born within the 'Adiprakriti', which is our original prakriti, into the transcendental realms with a 'cit-anand' body that is made up of bliss-consciousness, i.e. Radhe–Krishna.

* This event, when the *jiva-atmas* take birth into Adiprakriti or transcendental realm and attain their eternally blissful (cit-anand) body, is also known as 'Maha Raas', which was performed by Lord Shree Krishna for the Gopis in *Dwapara Yuga.*

* Bliss awareness breaks down only into 'cit' and 'Anand'. There is no 'SAT' present in the bliss body; therefore, 'Radha–Krishna' is also known as *'Chidanand' Swaroopam.*

* Bliss Consciousness (Radha–Krishna) exists independent of absolute consciousness (Laxmi–Narayan) and pure consciousness (Shiva–Shakti).

* In the transcendental realms, we have bliss consciousness that is made up of bliss awareness which helps us to perceive Adiprakriti and experience Super love (Radha).

* To enter the transcendental realms, we have to go beyond all concepts of physical existence or limitations, i.e. SAT, and exist only with our subtle body (Cit/consciousness) and causal body (Ananda/bliss). Actually, in the transcendental realm, there is only one common 'SAT' or Truth for all beings, and that is 'super love'.

* In the transcendental realm, we have 'Chidanand' swaroop, which also means that there are only waking and dreaming states. 'Cit' manifests itself as the waking state, and 'Ananda' manifests itself as the dreaming state of the bliss consciousness. This literally means that 'lovers' never go to sleep because there is no sleeping state within the bliss consciousness. For example, the

idol of Lord Jagannath is represented without any eyelids, which signifies that the supreme Lord always remains in the waking state of Bliss.

❖ There is no role of destruction in the transcendental realms because there remains only Adishakti or Radha, i.e. Super Love, who creates everything in the form of 'Cit', and there is Adipurush or Krsna, i.e. Super Bliss, who preserves everything that is created out of Super Love by Adishakti (Radha) in the form of 'Anand'.

❖ **Spiritual Principle**: The 'Subjective reality' always remains unaffected and independent of its 'object reality'.

For example: The rays of the Sun fall on all good and bad objects of the earth, but the sun does not get pure or impure as a result and always remains unaffected in its position.

Similarly,

(a) The 'mind' is the subjective reality that remains unaffected and independent of the actions that are performed by our 'bodies' which is its objective reality. Therefore, we can say that those who become free from their physical ego or material consciousness also become free from all the sinful or pious reactions of their actions or karmas.

(b) The 'soul' is the subjective reality that remains unaffected and independent of the thoughts produced by our 'mind' which is its objective reality. Therefore, we can say those who become free from their mind (subtle consciousness) remain untouched or unaffected by any positive or negative thoughts and become free from all sorts of illusions or *Maya*.

PARAM PURUSH AND PARAM PRAKRITI

- 'Narayana' is known as 'Param Purusha', and he is the unmanifested form of 'Infinity', i.e. 'Satchidanand'. He is the *subject* of infinity that is eternal and inexhaustible.
- 'Laxmi' is known as 'Param Prakriti', and she is the manifested form of 'Infinity', i.e. 'abundance', 'prosperity', and 'fortune'. She is the *object* of infinity that is also eternal and inexhaustible.
- Manifested Infinity = Eternal Time.
- Unmanifested Infinity = Eternal Space.
- 'Infinity' is made up of 'absolute consciousness'. Therefore, to understand infinity in a better way, we must first address a very basic but important question:

Q.) What do you mean by Consciousness and Awareness?
- Anything that occupies space and has awareness is known as 'Consciousness'. Just like we have matter, which is made up of atoms, similarly, we also have anti-matter, with the help of which we can perceive matter. This anti-matter is actually our 'consciousness' made up of anti-atoms that

can be understood as 'awareness'. Therefore, we can say 'Awareness' is the smallest unit of 'consciousness' which retains all the spiritual properties of a being. In our Apara Prakriti, we have 'Pure Consciousness' that is made of Pure awareness, which helps us to perceive matter and experience material reality. Similarly, in Param or Para Prakriti, we have 'Absolute Consciousness' that is made of absolute awareness, which helps us to perceive spirits and experience spiritual reality.

And just like our atoms at last break down into electrons, protons, and neutron, similarly, absolute awareness fundamentally breaks down into SAT (being), Cit (consciousness), and Ananda (bliss).

* ❖ 'SAT' (being) manifests itself as the 'Eternal Waking state' of absolute consciousness;
* ❖ 'Cit' (consciousness) manifests itself as the 'Eternal Dreaming State' of absolute consciousness, and
* ❖ 'Anand' (bliss) manifests itself as the 'Eternal Sleeping state' of absolute consciousness.
* ❖ SAT, CIT, and ANAND diagram:

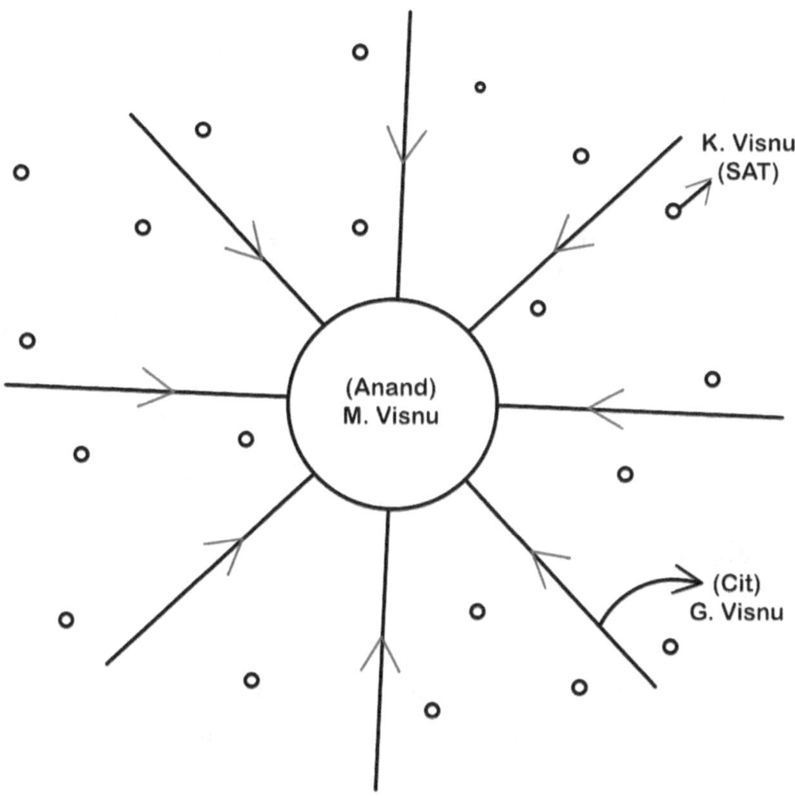

- ❖ Narayana manifests himself in the eternal waking state as 'SAT' (being) and is known as 'Ksirodakshayi Vishnu'. As K. Vishnu, he's the 'Creator' and knower of absolute reality, and is also known as 'Parameshwara' or 'God'.
- ❖ Narayana manifests himself in the eternal dreaming state as 'Cit' (consciousness) and is known as 'Garbhodakshayi Vishnu'. As G. Vishnu, he is the 'preserver' and knowledge of absolute reality, and is also known as 'Param Atma' or 'Super Soul'.
- ❖ Narayana manifests himself in the eternal sleeping state as 'Ananda' (bliss) and is known as 'Maha-Vishnu'. As

M. Vishnu, he is the 'destroyer' and known of absolute reality, and is also known as 'Param Brahm' or 'Super Brahman'.

Q.) How does absolute consciousness work or function?

- From the diagram of 'Sacchianand', we can clearly see that in the absolute consciousness there is only one bliss, that is, 'M. Vishnu' or 'Param Brahman'. In the Vedas, M. Vishnu (Param Brahman) is depicted in the Sleeping state or position. And it is also mentioned in our Vedas that M. Vishnu is without any beginning or end, which means he is infinite and also has no specific shape or form. Therefore, we can say that in the absolute consciousness, the nature of our subject or the subjective reality is 'Formlessness'. (The subject always remains singular and unmanifested, but the object manifests itself in duality as unmanisfested and manifested object).

And as we know that objective reality always exists in duality, we can say that 'G. Vishnu' or 'Param Atma' acts as the unmanifested object, that is, 'spiritual knowledge', with the help of which he preserves absolute reality.

Now, the Param Atma (G. Vishnu) further expands himself into multiple gods and goddesses, where he manifests himself as 'K. Vishnu', i.e. manifested object, and acts as the creator of absolute reality and is also known as 'Parameshwar'.

In simple words, we can say that the Param Atma (G. Vishnu) gives birth to multiple spirits as 'K. Vishnu', who manifests himself within all gods and goddesses. And all of these gods or goddesses being manifestations of absolute objective reality ultimately revolves around one subject that is absolute and formless bliss, also known as Param Brahman (M. Vishnu).

❖ Param or Para Prakriti (Laxmi) is the object of 'infinity' that is also eternal and inexhaustible. She represents prosperity, abundance, and fortune. She also manifests herself along with her subject (satcitanand) or husband (Param Purush) into the three states of absolute consciousness as follows:

i. Laxmi or 'Para Prakriti' manifests herself as 'Sandhini Shakti', i.e. infinite knowledge, thereby making Parameshwar (K. Visnu) 'omniscient' in the waking state of absolute consciousness, i.e. SAT. As unlimited knowledge or wisdom, she is the creator of absolute reality and also sustains our spiritual or divine physical body.

ii. Laxmi or 'Para Prakriti' manifests herself as 'Sambit Shakti', i.e. infinite power, thereby making Param Atma (G. Vishnu) 'omnipotent' in the dreaming state of absolute consciousness, i.e. Cit. As unlimited power or potential, she is the preserver of absolute reality and also sustains our spiritual or divine subtle body.

iii. Laxmi or 'Para Prakriti' manifests herself as 'Hladini Shakti', i.e. infinite awareness, making Param Brahman (M. Vishnu) 'omnipresent' in the sleeping state of absolute consciousness, i.e. Anand. As unlimited awareness, she is the destroyer of absolute reality and also sustains our spiritual or divine causal body.

❖ There is Illusion (Maya) in absolute reality as well, but this illusion can never overpower the spirits or Gods; instead, the illusion (Maya) becomes controlled or manipulated by the spirits or gods, i.e. (K. Vishnu), through yoga or union with Maya. That is why, in absolute reality, 'Maya' becomes 'Yoga-Maya', which means illusion that is in full control of her master, i.e. Param Purusha (Narayan).

❖ We can also understand Laxmi–Narayan, i.e. 'absolute consciousness', as the link or bridge that connects Shiva–Shakti, i.e. 'pure consciousness', with Radha–Krishna, i.e. 'bliss consciousness'. That is why, in our Sanatan philosophy, 'Vishnu' is also known as the god of liberation and bestower of 'Moksha'. Lord Narayana is known for providing an unsinkable boat to his devotees with the help of which they can cross the ocean of illusion (Maya) and reach their ultimate destination, that is, into Bliss Consciousness, where there is no illusion (Maya) or lies but only one common or universal truth, that is, 'Super Love' (Radha).

❖ In Param Purusha (Narayan) - Subject

Param Brahm - Unmanifest
Param atma - Manifest
Param ishwar - Manifest

❖ In Para Prakriti (Laxmi) - Object
   Unlimited awareness - Unmanifest
   Unlimited Power - Manifest
   Unlimited knowledge - Manifest

PURUSH AND PRAKRITI

- ❖ 'Shiva' is known as 'Purusha', and he is the unmanifested form or subject of nothingness (shunya), that is, 'Space'. He is also eternal in nature but exhaustible, which makes the painful process of change and transformation inevitable for *purusha*.

- ❖ 'Shakti' is known as 'Prakriti', and she is the manifested form or object of nothingness (shunya), that is, 'Time'. She is eternal but exhaustible as well, due to which *prakriti* is also required to go through the painful process of change and transformation.

- ❖ Shiva–Shakti together is also known as pure consciousness. Therefore, we can also say that what we call as nothingness is simply 'pure consciousness'.

- ❖ 'Pure Consciousness', i.e. Nothingness, is the equal and opposite reaction of 'absolute consciousness', i.e. Infinity. This means Brahm or nothingness (Shiva) and Param Brahm or infinity (Narayan) balance each other and are dependent on each other for their survival as one cannot exist without the other.

- ❖ Actually, Bliss Consciousness (Paramanand) is the subject; therefore, it exists independently and remains 'unmanifested'; whereas Absolute Consciousness (Infinity) and Pure Consciousness (Nothingness) are the object of Bliss Consciousness; therefore, they have to manifest by existing in duality and have to maintain the balance between them. This is why, in Sanatan dharma, we believe that Lord Vishnu takes avatar as an incarnation of Narayan in every Yuga on earth to re-establish the balance between 'dharma', that is, absolute consciousness and 'Adharma', that is, pure consciousness.

❖ Let us also understand the relationship between Pure Consciousness, Absolute Consciousness, and Bliss Consciousness with the help of the following diagram:

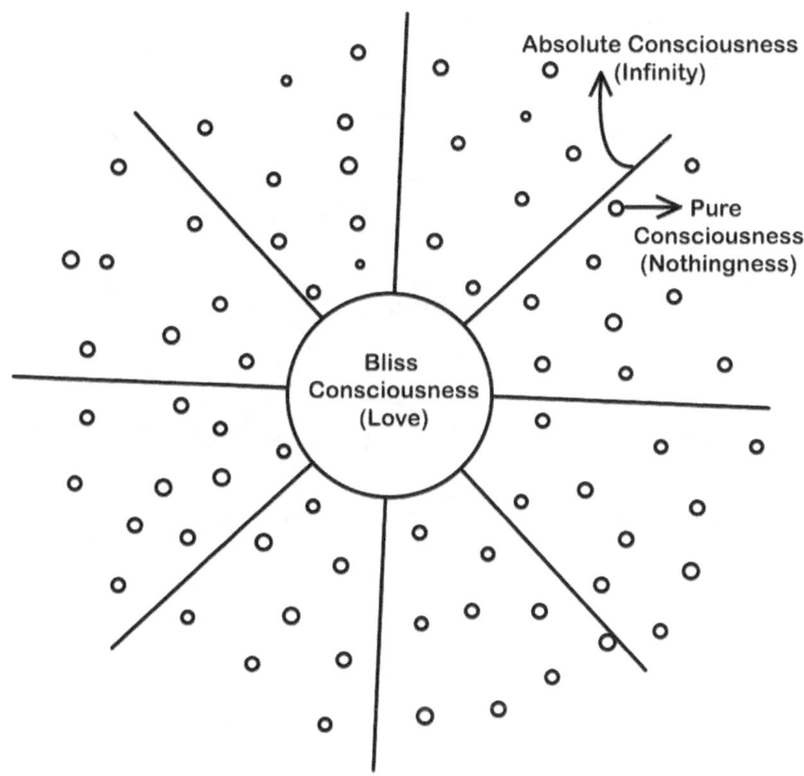

- ❖ Param Purasha (Narayan) manifests as 'Satcitanand' in the absolute consciousness, whereas Purusha (Shiva) manifests itself as exactly the opposite of 'Satcitanand' in Pure consciousness, which means:

- ❖ 'SAT' (Truth/Nitya) becomes 'ASAT' (False/Anitya), 'CIT' (Consciousness/Spirit) becomes 'JADD' (Unconscious/Matter), and 'ANAND' (Bliss) becomes 'DUKHA' (Pain and Suffering).

- ❖ 'Asat', 'Jadd', and 'Dukha' diagram:

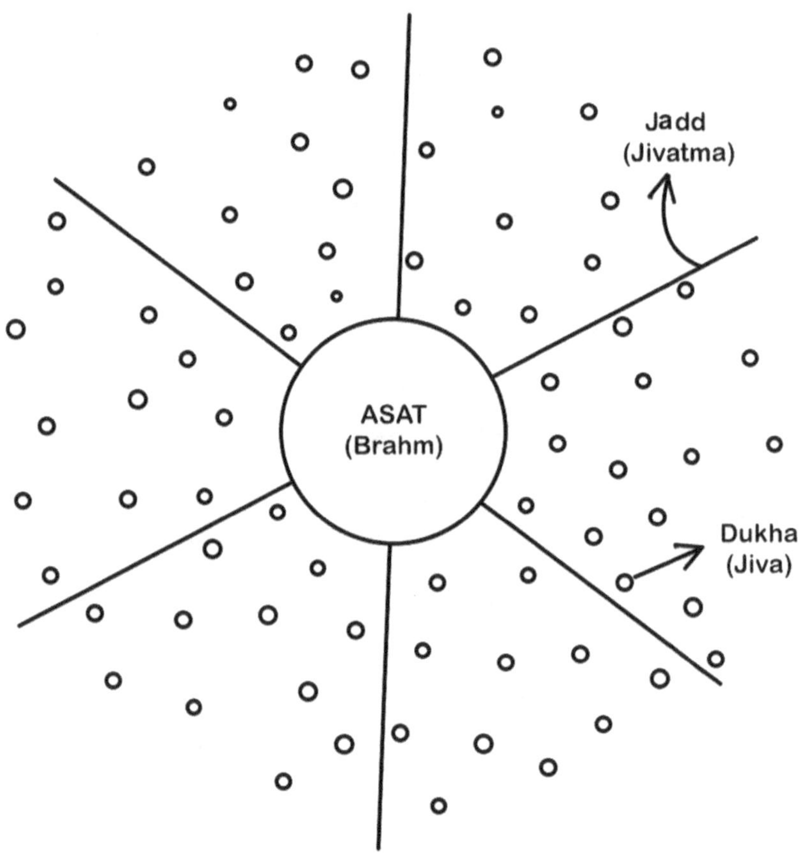

1) Shiva (Purusha) manifests himself as 'Swayambhu' or 'Sada-Siva' in the waking state of Pure Consciousness, i.e. (ASAT), also known as 'Brahman'. As Brahm, he is the creator and knower of Pure Consciousness.

2) Shiva (Purusha) manifests himself as 'Shankara' in the dreaming state of Pure Consciousness, i.e. (JADD), also known as 'Jivatma'. As jivatma, he is the preserver and knowledge of Pure Consciousness.

3) Shiva (Purusha) manifests himself as 'Rudra' in the sleeping state of Pure Consciousness, i.e. (DUKHA), also known as 'Jiva'. As jiva, he is the destroyer and 'Known' of Pure Consciousness.

❖ Now, Prakriti (Shakti) is the manifested form or object of nothingness and is also known as 'Time' or 'Kaali'. She also manifests herself into the three states of Pure Consciousness along with her subject, i.e. Purusha (Shiva).

1) 'Prakriti' manifests herself into the sleeping state of pure consciousness, i.e. *dukha*, as 'Ma' and gives birth to our physical body, i.e. *Jiva*. It is sustained with food, and when jiva (physical body) becomes awakened through yogic practices, it can develop the ability to differentiate between good and bad food. As Ma, she is the destroyer of pure consciousness.

2) 'Prakriti' manifests herself as 'Maya' in the dreaming state of pure consciousness, i.e. jadd and gives birth to our subtle body, i.e. Jiva-atma. It is sustained with knowledge, and when jiva-atma becomes awakened

through yogic practices, it can develop the ability to differentiate between positive or negative thoughts, i.e. Vivek (discretion). As Maya, she is the preserver of pure consciousness.

3) 'Prakriti' manifests herself as the force of life, i.e. 'Shakti', in the waking state of pure consciousness, i.e. ASAT, and gives birth to our causal body, i.e. Brahm. And it is sustained with space, and when brahm becomes awakened, it can develop the ability to differentiate between good or bad desires and Karmas (actions). As Shakti, she is the creator of pure consciousness.

The main job of Prakriti is to provide us with a separate platform that can help us understand Para Prakriti so that we can transcend it because it is not possible for us to transcend Para Prakriti while we are in it, i.e. absolute consciousness. For example, to fetch water from the well we can't jump into the well but have to fetch it from outside the well, similarly, in order for us to understand and transcend Para Prakriti, we are sent into Apara Prakriti to learn through our own experiences and then rise above both Para and Apara Prakriti and ultimately manifest ourselves into our original Adiprakriti, i.e. Super Love.

In other words, Apara Prakriti or 'pure consciousness' is a platform that is outside the well of 'Para Prakriti' or 'absolute consciousness'. Our bodies are like buckets which are thrown into the well or pool of absolute consciousness through the ropes of spiritual practices. And depending upon its own capacity, a soul manages to fetch some water out of the pool or well of absolute consciousness that subsequently evaporates into 'Adiprakriti' or bliss consciousness as the temperature of our love for Krsna, i.e Super Bliss, rises, and that's how we transcend both Apara and Para Prakriti.

Q.) How does Pure Consciousness work or function?

- From the diagram of 'ASAT, JADD, and DUKHA' we can say that in the pure consciousness there is one Brahman (sada shiva), i.e. 'ASAT' or 'False' or Anitya.

In Sanatan dharma, 'Shiva linga' is worshipped by Hindus for thousands of years because it is the symbol that represents nothingness (Shiva) in his waking state, that is, 'Brahman' or 'sada-shiva', and because in this waking state or as brahman he is the creator of our universe, by worshipping its symbol, that is, shiva linga, all of our material desires or wishes get fulfilled. As per our scriptures, 'Brahman' or 'sada-shiva' is also known as 'Swayambhu', which means he is self-manifested and is without any beginning or end. Therefore, we can say that 'Brahm' is also eternal and infinite as it has no specific shape or form. And we can also conclude that the nature of our subject or subjective reality of pure consciousness is 'Formless'.

Now that we have discussed the nature of our subject or subjective reality of pure consciousness, i.e. Brahman, let us now discuss our objectives that exist in duality, meaning 'Brahm' (ASAT) expands itself further as 'Jiva-atma', i.e. jadd, which acts as an unmanifested object, and it finally expands itself into multiple 'Jivas', i.e. Dukha, which create the manifested objective reality of pure consciousness.

❖ Many people who ask why there is so much pain and suffering in this world and doubt the abilities of the creator should know that, in Pure Consciousness, pain and suffering are inevitable because that is what it is made of as we can clearly see from the diagram of 'Pure consciousness'. In fact, Jiva, i.e. our physical body, itself is the origin of all our pain and suffering because all these Jivas or Rudras, i.e. physical body, are manifested out of the pain and suffering of labour.

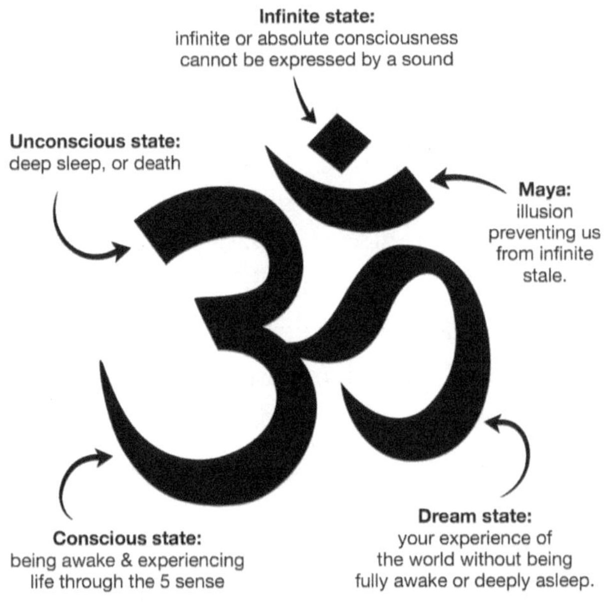

❖ Now that we have learned quite a bit about Bliss, Absolute, and Pure Consciousness we can say:

RADHA, i.e. Super Love, is an eternal being that has three eternal states of consciousness that are as follows:

(i) <u>Pure Consciousness</u>

This is the sleeping state of 'Super Love' in which our eternity is spent with the chaos and suffering of transformations. It is mainly concerned with harnessing the power of destruction through which it can make us forget our connection with almighty and take away the seeds of pure love that we all inherently have for him. In simple words, 'Pure Consciousness' is actually our 'Eternal Hell'.

(ii) <u>Absolute Consciousness</u>

This is the dreaming state of 'Super Love' in which our eternity is spent with the peace and power of knowledge. It is mainly concerned with the preservation of the super love or faith that we inherently have for the almighty. In simple words, we can say that 'Absolute Consciousness' is our 'Eternal Heaven'.

(iii) <u>Bliss consciousness</u>

This is the waking state of 'Super Love' in which our eternity is spent with the bliss and love of Krsna. It is mainly concerned with the creation or enhancement of the super love that we all inherently have for Lord Krsna. In simple words, we can say that 'Bliss Consciousness' is our actual or original home where there is the 'Eternal kingdom of supreme God', which is beyond heaven and hell. That is why, in Sanatan dharma, Hindus are prescribed by the Rasik saints to renounce the desire for all kinds of Muktis/Moksha, i.e. Heaven, as well as renounce all our desires for pleasure from Bhukti/Bhoga, i.e. Hell, and accept only unconditional 'Super Love' for Radhe–Krsna as our ultimate destination and supreme goal.

❖ From Purusha (Shiva) - Subject
(Causal body) Brahm - Unmanifest
(Subtle body) Jiva-atma - Manifest
(Physical body) Jiva - Manifest

❖ From Prakriti (Time of Shakti) - Object
(Energy) Shakti - Unmanifest
(Illusion) Maya - Manifest
(Nature) Ma - Manifest

❖ Time, i.e. Prakriti, is the consciousness of space, i.e. Purusha. We can think of time like an ocean in which past, present, and future are like the waves of ocean that create movement on the surface of time (Prakriti).

The manifestation of past, present, and future occurs only at the surface of time, i.e. Third Dimension, where everything is changing into past, present, and future. It seems like the waves of ocean interacting with each other in the form of our past, present, and future. But here at the surface of time our destinies are fixed, which means, in the 3rd dimension, we can't change our past, present, or future as it would appear to be fixed or destined at the surface level of time.

But as we go or dive deeper into time or Prakriti that is into the 4th dimension we get access to unmanifested time, i.e. causal body, which is like a clean slate, that is, free from all the memories of our past, present, or future. And there is no movement or stillness in the 4th dimension of time, and it is the place from where we are allowed to rewrite or recreate our destiny by redefining our past, present, and future.

It is mentioned in our scriptures as well that 'Yama', who is the god of death, and 'Chitragupt', his assistant who keeps the track record of all our actions, also live in the 4th dimension of time. And even after our death we are taken into the 4th dimension, i.e. Yam-loka, where we receive reward or punishment according to our good and bad actions (Karmas).

❖ Just like light and matter show dual nature, that is, 'Particle' and 'Wave', similarly, the soul (Atman) also shows dual nature, that is, 'Personal' (Particle) and 'Impersonal' (Wave).

❖ The Soul (Atman) only shows its personal or particle form when it is in its 'sleeping state', impersonal or wave form in its 'dreaming state', and, at last, the soul (atman) achieves the ability or freedom to switch between both personal and impersonal forms at will in its 'waking state'.

❖ If we look at our mind, i.e. jivatma, from the 'Jiva' or Physical Egos perspective, then it appears to be formless or attribute-less because it is acting as a subject here and thus gives birth to atheist or *advait* school of philosophy.

❖ But if we look at our mind from the 'Brahm' or Soul's perspective, then it is made up of three gunas, i.e. Sattva,

Rajas, and Tamas, because it is acting as an object here, and we already know that object always exists in duality. Similarly, if we look at our Super Mind (Paramatma) from the God's point of view, that is, subjective perspective, then it is formless; however, if we look at it from the Param Brahman's point of view, that is, objective perspective, then it is also made up of three gunas, i.e. Para Sattva, Para Rajas, and Para Tamas. In Bhagwat Gita, Lord Krishna analyses the mind from the Soul's (Brahman) point of view and therefore explains only the three gunas in detail, but in this book we will go even further and also analyze our Super Mind (paramatma) from the highest perspective of Param or Super Brahman, along with all the six gunas of both Para and Apara Prakriti in our next chapter.

SIX GUNAS OF PARA AND APARA PRAKRITI

❖ 'Prakriti' is like a shiny object or mirror-like tool that is used by 'Purusha' to see its own reflection and realise or remember his true nature that is one with the supreme Lord. And just like a mirror absorbs the light from an object and reflects its image, similarly, Prakriti (Time) absorbs the spiritual light from Purusha (Space) and simply reflects its image. For example:

❖ In Pure Consciousness:

Purush	-	Prakriti
(Brahm) Asat	-	Sattva guna
(Jivatma) Jadd	-	Rajas guna
(Jiva) Dukha	-	Tamas guna

1) **Sattva-guna**

(a) Prakriti absorbs the light from our causal body or Brahman, i.e. Asat/Anitya, and reflects it as 'Sattva-guna'. It is responsible for the force of creation in Prakriti.

   (b) 'Sattva' is actually our 'Thoughts' about which we can say that all our thoughts are nothing but simply the reflection or image of Brahman (causal body) within us, i.e. 'ASAT'. Therefore, we can say that all our thoughts are also simply illusion or unreal.

   (c) When 'Brahm' is in its dormant or unconscious state in our body, it becomes almost impossible for us to control our thoughts. But if Brahman is awakened within us with the help of yoga, then we can gain the ability to control or direct the flow of our thoughts and even make it stop which can lead us to experience the state of mental absorption or Samadhi, i.e. 'Thoughtless State'.

   (d) All our thoughts flow by the power or Shakti of Brahman; therefore, spiritual masters have said that our thoughts are very powerful because they are carrying the energy of Brahman within them. And therefore those who can learn to gain the control over their thoughts can easily utilize or harness the power of their awareness, in turn enhancing their productivity and creativity skills.

2) **Rajas-guna**

   (a) Prakriti absorbs the light from our subtle body or Jivatma, i.e. JADD or unconscious/matter, and reflects it as 'Rajas-guna'. It is responsible for the force of preservation in Prakriti.

   (b) 'Rajas-guna' is actually our doubts and fears that are reflected due to the presence of Jiva-atma (subtle body) within us because it is 'jadd' or unconscious. Therefore, we can say all of our doubts and fears are simply manifestation of rajas-guna that arises out of the unconscious/jadd nature of our subtle body, i.e. 'Jiva-atma'.

(c) When 'Jivaatma' or subtle body is dormant or unawakened, our life becomes miserable and full of doubts and fears. But if it is awakened or made conscious with the help of yoga, then it can overcome all the doubts or lack of faith that arises out of the unconscious or jadd nature of rajas-guna, gain absolute clarity about everything in life, and become fearless.

(d) The Jivatma or subtle body operates through the energy of Maya (illusion); therefore, we can say all our doubts are also made of illusion and has nothing to do with the ultimate truth. That is why, we don't need to entertain them and are required to rise above all these unnecessary doubts so that we can accomplish our ultimate goal, that is, to first understand the nature of absolute reality and then transcend it into super blissful reality.

3) <u>Tamas-guna</u>

(a) Prakriti absorbs the light from our physical body or Jiva, i.e. dhuka (pain and suffering) and then reflects it as 'Tamas-guna'. It is responsible for the force of destruction in Prakriti.

(b) Tamas-guna is actually our desires that are reflected

due to the presence of 'jiva', that is, pain or suffering within us. Therefore, we can say that all our desires are simply manifestations of Tamas-guna that arises out of the pain or sufferings of 'jiva' or the physical body.

(c) When 'Jiva' or physical body is in a dormant or unawakened state, life becomes very restless and filled of desires. But if the jiva or physical body is awakened or made conscious with the practice of yoga, then it can easily control or restrain all its unnecessary desires that are harmful for the jiva (physical body) and gain mastery or control over his or her senses.

(d) 'Jiva' or physical body operates through the energy of 'Ma', i.e. material nature; therefore, we can say that the nature of all our desires are also materialistic and lead to bondage or attachment with the material nature. Thus, in order for us to evolve spiritually, it is recommended by the masters to renounce all our desires that ultimately lead to bondage with illusion (Maya).

❖ Diagram - Apara Prakriti

(Sun)

The Sun (Sattva) is the reflection of 'Brahman'
that creates of our Causal body.

(Moon)

The Moon (Rajas) is the reflection of
'Jivatma' that creates our Subtle body.

The earth (Tamas) is the reflection of 'Jiva'
that creates our Physical body.

❖ In absolute Consciousness:

Param Purusha		Para Prakriti
(Parameshwar) SAT	→	Para Sattva
(Param-Atma) Cit	→	Para Rajas
(Param-Brahm) Anand	→	Para Tamas

1) <u>Para Sattva:</u>

(a) Para Prakriti absorbs spiritual or divine light from our spiritual body or 'Parameshwar' (God), i.e. 'SAT', and reflects it as 'Para Sattva'. It is responsible for the force of creation in Para Prakriti. It is by the virtue of Para Sattva that the Lord is also known as 'Atma-Kridah', which means the one who is sporting or playing in the atma or spirit self.

(b) 'Para Sattva' is actually the Guru-Tattva that gives us the ability of being omniscient. Para Sattva or 'Guru-Tattva' is the manifestation of divine or infinite spiritual knowledge that comes directly from Parameshwar (God). That is why guru is often compared as equal or even greater than God because he is, in fact, is a tool through which God really expresses himself.

(c) Para Sattva (Guru-Tattva) is the object that revolves around its subject, that is, Parameshwar (God). That's why those who have developed this divine guna often like to talk about God all the time and also possess vast spiritual knowledge.

(d) Just like we can see our reflection on a shiny object like mirror, similarly, to see the reflection of Parameshwar

(God) we need the help of guru or Para Sattva who has the absolute purity of consciousness on which God reflects himself as SAT (being), i.e. 'omniscient'.

2) <u>Para-Rajas:</u>

a) Para Prakriti absorbs the spiritual light from our divine subtle body or Param-atma (Super Soul), i.e. consciousness (Cit), and reflects it as 'Para Rajas'. It is responsible for the force of preservation in Para Prakriti.

b) 'Para-Rajas' is actually the 'Superhuman Tattva' that gives us unlimited spiritual potential or power that can make us omnipotent. It is the 'Superhuman Tattva' on which Param-Atma (Super Soul) manifests his divine powers, i.e. siddhis, and makes such a person extraordinarily great.

c) Para-Rajas (Superhuman Tattva) is the object or tool through which Param-Atma (Supersoul) expresses himself as CIT (consciousness), i.e. 'omnipotent'.

d) It is by the virtue of Para Rajas that the Lord is also known as 'Atma-Ratih', meaning the one who is delighted in the atma or spirit self.

For example, 'Hanuman ji' is the manifestation of Para Rajas on which Param Atma (Ram) reflects his quality of omnipotence or unlimited potential perfectly.

3) <u>Para Tamas:</u>

a.) Para Prakriti absorbs the spiritual light from our divine causal body or Param Brahm (Super Brahman), i.e. Bliss (Ananda), and reflects it as 'Para Tamas'. It is responsible for the force of destruction in Para Prakriti.

b.) 'Para Tamas' is kind of a Mystical Tattva to understand as it gives one the power of being present everywhere at all times, also known as ' omnipresence'. It is rather the 'Bliss Tattva' that is very mystical in nature and is reflected due to the presence of unlimited or infinite awareness in Param Brahman, i.e. (M. Vishnu).

c.) For example, Srimad Bhagvatam narrates an incident when Lord Krsna showed his ability of being present at multiple places simultaneously, i.e. 'omnipresence', to Narada Muni. Once, when Narada visits Dwarka, he sees Lord Krsna being present and interacting with all his 16,108 queens at the same time and was very much astonished.

d.) It is by the virtue of Para Tamas that the Lord is also known as 'Atma-Rama'. which means the one who takes pleasure in the atma or spirit self.

Diagram: Para Prakriti

(Spiritual Sun)
(Saket-Loka)

(Spiritual Moon)
(kailash)

(Spiritual Earth)
or
(Vaikunth Loka)

(Spiritual Sun) (Saket/Ram-loka): Spiritual Sun (P. Tamas) is the reflection of P. Brahm (Super Brahman) that exists in the spiritual sky and creates our divine 'causal body'.

Spiritual Moon (Kailash/Shiv-loka): Spiritual Moon (P. Rajas) is the reflection of P. Atma (Super Soul) that exists in the spiritual sky and creates our divine 'Subtle body'.

Spiritual Earth (Vaikunth/Vishnu-loka): Spiritual Earth (P. Sattva) is the reflection of Parameshwar (God) that exists in the spiritual sky and creates our divine physical, i.e. 'spiritual body'.

* ***Diagram of 6- Gunas:***

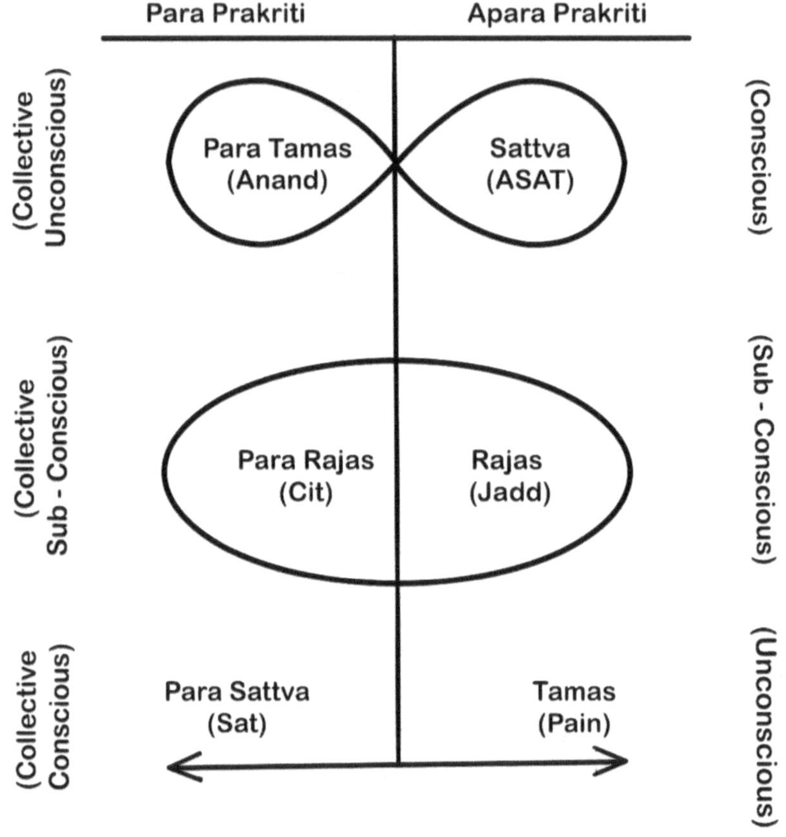

a) All the 6 gunas of Para and Apara Prakriti together form the image of the sacred number '108'.

b) 'Para Tamas', i.e. Anand, reflects itself as 'Sattva', i.e. ASAT, in the Apara Prakriti, meaning all our thoughts are simply projections of unlimited awareness, i.e. bliss (Anand), which is hidden within all of us as Super Brahman. Thoughts are like clouds that hide the bliss of Sun, i.e. Super Brahman. We can also say that the conscious mind that is made of Sattva-gun (ASAT) is the reflection of collective unconscious state of mind that is made of Para Tamas (Anand). All things in creation that are infinite and countless are due to 'Para Tamas' and 'Sattva', such as hair on our head, stars in the sky, etc.

(c) 'Para Rajas' (Cit/consciousness) reflects itself as 'Rajas' (jadd/unconsciousness) in the Apara Prakriti, which means all our doubts and fears are simply projections of unlimited potential, i.e. consciousness (cit), which is present within all of us. 'Param-Atma' is like the Sun of unlimited potential or power that is hidden behind the clouds of our 'doubts and fears'. We can also say that the subconscious state of mind which is made of Rajas-gun, i.e. jadd, is the reflection of collective subconscious state of mind that is made from Para Rajas, i.e. cit. All cyclic or circular motions in our creation are due to Rajas and Para Rajas, such as Earth revolving around the Sun, moon revolving around the earth, etc.

d.) 'Para Sattva' (SAT) reflects itself as 'Tamas' (Pain) in the Apara Prakriti, which means all our desires are simply projections of the unlimited knowledge, i.e. being (SAT), that exists within all of us. 'Parameshwar' or God is also like the Sun of infinite knowledge that is hidden behind the clouds of our 'desires'. We can also say that the unconscious state of our mind which is made of Tamas-gun, i.e. pain, is the reflection of collective conscious state of mind that is made of 'Para Sattva', i.e. being. All things in creation that can be individualized are due to Tamas and Para Sattva, such as our identities, countries, cultures, etc.

Para Sattva	Tamas
Collective conscious (unity/being)	Individual or unconscious (ego/pain)
Mindful	Oblivious
Absolute purity	Impurity
Equality	Division or discrimination
Constructive power	Destructive power
Empathy	Narcissism
Absolute truth	Delusion
Omniscience	Ignorance
Bright or brilliance	Dullness
Contentment or desirelessness	Discontentment or desireful
Calm and forgiving	Angry and vengeful
Respectful and humility	Arrogance and pride

Para Tamas	Sattva
Collective unconscious (purity of thoughts)	Conscious (impurity of thoughts)
Spiritual bliss (inexhaustible)	Material bliss (exhaustible)
Infinity	Nothingness
Expansion	Reduction
Unification	Dissolution
Total detachment from self	Attachment to self
Unlimited awareness (omnipresence)	Limited awareness (bounded)

Para Rajas	Rajas
Omnipotence	Impotence
Equanimity	Anxious
Generous	Greedy
Compassionate	Passionate
Discernment and discretion	Stupidity and indecisiveness
Collective subconscious (harmony and peace)	Subconscious (chaos and transformation)
Absolute clarity	Doubtful
Unwavering peace	Disturbed
Sense of completeness	Emptiness
In control	Out of control
Fearless	Fearful

❖ **In Apara Prakriti:**

1) **Sattva-gun has three states:**

   a) **Waking State:** Peaceful, clarity, strong memory, informative, liberal, cautious, humility, loyalty, honesty, etc.

   b) **Dreaming State:** Positive thoughts, religious, disciplined, charitable, organized, punctual, etc.

   c) **Deep Sleep:** Lack of imagination, forgetfulness, non-believer, atheist, lack of empathy, immaturity, distrustful, thug, etc.

2) <u>Rajas-gun has three states:</u>

   a) <u>**Waking State:**</u> Highly ambitious, assertive, motivated, driven, workaholic, etc.

   b) <u>**Dreaming state**</u>: Doubtful, unsatisfied, quarrelsome, fearful, lustful, selfish, self- centred, competitive etc.

   c) <u>**Deep Sleep**</u>: Lack of motivation, no goals, cowardice, obsession, disoriented, restlessness, anxious, etc.

3) <u>Tamas-gun has three states:</u>

   a) <u>**Waking State**</u>: Stability, consistency, rigid or orthodox beliefs, patience, ignorance, tolerance etc.

   b) <u>**Dreaming State**</u>: Negative intention, perversion, violent, hurtful, traumatic, vengeful, etc.

   c) <u>**Deep Sleep**</u>: Highly narcissistic, cruel, numbness, lethargic, evil, deep suffering, sorrowful, depression, etc.

The fourth and common state of all three gunas is known as ' Pure Consciousness', i.e. Shiv–Shakti.

❖ <u>**In Para Prakriti:**</u>

1) Para Sattva also has three states:

   a) <u>**Waking State**</u>: Saint, guru, omniscient, empathy, mindful, gratitude, positive thinking, clairvoyance, Atma-Kridah, etc.

   b) <u>**Dreaming State**</u>: Mantra, rituals, renunciation, devotion, brilliance, etc.

c) **Deep Sleep**: Idols, devotees, surrender, absolute purity, etc.

2) Para Rajas also has three states:

a) **Waking State**: Absolute awareness, omnipotence, absolute clarity, Superhuman skills, clairaudience, Atma-Ratih, etc.

b) **Dreaming State**: Equanimity, desireless deeds or *non-doership*, discernment, fearless, harmony, compassion, etc.

c) **Deep Sleep**: Curiosity or thirst for knowledge, discretion, spiritual books, generous, etc.

3) Para Tamas has three states as well:

a) **Waking State**: Infinite or inexhaustible bliss, immortality, omnipresence, clairsentience, *Nirvikalp Samadhi*, Atma-Rama, etc.

b) **Dreaming State**: Infinity, expansion, unification, meditation, mysticism, etc.

c) **Deep Sleep:** Detachment, formlessness, Brahmacharya, *Savikalp Samadhi*, etc.

The fourth and common state of all three gunas is known as 'Absolute Consciousness', i.e. Laxmi–Narayan.

TYPES OF MIND

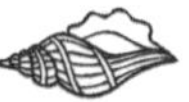

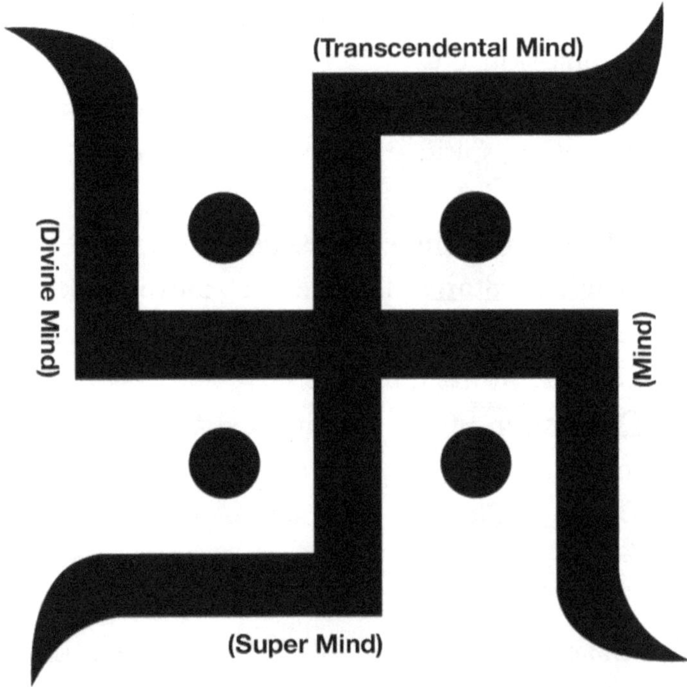

1) Mind (Apara Prakriti)

Mind is a vehicle that is made up of pure consciousness through which 'Purusha' explores 'Prakriti'. It is a manifested gadget or tool that exists between the two polarities of unmanifested reality, that is, beginning (life) and ending (death). Mind (vehicle) starts its journey from Apara Prakriti and also terminates somewhere in Apara Prakriti, which means that the mind is a vehicle that is born out of material nature (Maya) and will also have its ending in material nature.

For example, just like our Ola or Uber cabs need pick-up and drop location to start your ride, similarly, our mind also needs two coordinates of space and time to start our journey of life, that is, our beginning or pick-up location (place and time of birth) and ending or drop location (place and time of death).

This vehicle of mind is made up of five layers or sheaths that is also known as 'Panch koshas' or five sheaths of our mind-:

i.	Anmay kosh	-	Physical body
ii.	Pranmay kosh	-	Intelligence body
iii.	Manomay kosh	-	Intellect body
iv.	Vigyanmay kosh	-	Samskara body
v.	Anandmay kosh	-	Chitta body

All the five bodies or *koshas* are like fragments of the whole, i.e. a super intelligent being that has been separated into different parts, but each has their own intelligence; therefore, there is a sense of incompleteness within all the five koshas or bodies. As a result of this longing to complete themselves or become whole again, they produce different types of ideas that manifest themselves in the form of different kinds of desires within all the bodies. But the problem is that all the five bodies have their own definitions of wholeness, or let's say, different versions of the truth. But because of the fact that they are only fragments of the whole, it is impossible for any single individual body (kosha) to comprehend the whole truth on its own, as their ability to perceive the whole truth has also been narrowed down. This indicates that they can only grasp a limited portion of the whole truth. It is only when all the five separate bodies combine their individual realizations or truths and put it together do they have a possibility to see the whole or complete truth as it is. For example:

i) For our Physical body, i.e. Anmay Kosh, immortality is the way to become whole or complete; therefore, it tries to preserve our physical body by producing desires to eat and reproduce.

ii) Our Intelligence body (Pranmay Kosh) believes that the only way to feel complete again is to ensure our own safety and survival. Therefore, it tries to keep us in our comfort zone and makes sure that our future is secured by learning from the mistakes or experiences of the past. All of our self-centred or selfish desires are born out of intelligence body that mainly deals with logics or has a logical sense of understanding.

iii) Our Intellect body (Manomay kosh) thinks that it is not possible to achieve the sense of completeness or wholeness on our own; therefore, it creates the ideas or concepts of having a family, community, club, state, country, etc. so that it can form new connections and maintain relationships with others. Thus, all the desires produced by our intellect body (manomay kosh) are mostly selfless and involve good will of others because it thinks in terms of collective conscience and mainly functions with the help of our intuitions or gut feelings.

iv) Our Samskara body (Vigyanmay Kosh) thinks of following routines, pattern, or structure as its idea of the whole and therefore tries to keep us consistent, systematic, orderly, and predictable, and basically stick to certain kind of uniformity in our lives. Thus, all our desires to follow any kind of system, routine, or pattern are simply born out of our 'Samskara body' (Vigyanmay kosh).

v) The Chitta body (Anandmay kosh) believes that if there is any such thing as a whole, then it must be chaotic, random, disorderly, unsystematic, unknowable, unpredictable, and irrational. All of our unconventional desires to do something out of the box or go out of the league to accomplish your goals arise from our Chitta body. Its main job is to push us outside our comfort zones by producing desires that are usually risky, reckless, and sometimes even unacceptable. These desires can be extremely good or extremely bad depending on the nature and past actions of the person; there is no in-between. If we start listening to or following all the desires that are produced by our Chitta body (Anandmay kosh), then it can either make us a 'superhero' or turn us into a 'supervillain' depending upon his or her good or bad nature and actions performed in the past. For example, the desires produced by Chitta may go from killing someone, taking your own life, doing something illegal, fighting, or rebelling to doing something extremely good like sacrificing your life for the nation, donating all your money to charity, saving the world, etc.; only extreme desires are produced here. The Chitta body (Anandmay kosh) gives the final push to our extreme desires that are also in accordance with or acceptable by our other four bodies or Koshas. If the other four bodies become weak and give up, only then the Chitta body is allowed to take over and subsequently impose its extremely good or bad desires on us and thus inspire us to venture into the unknown. The main role of the Chitta body is to break the monotony of desires that are produced by other four bodies by bringing chaos, disorder, and randomness. That's why, in Bhagwat Gita, Lord Krishna said to Arjuna that the Chitta (Anandmay kosh) is the greatest benefactor for those who are good in nature and perform pious deeds and is the greatest enemy for those who are evil by nature and indulge in the sinful acts of crime.

2) Divine Mind (Para Prakriti):

The divine Mind is a vehicle that is made up of absolute consciousness through which 'Param Purusha' explores or travels in 'Para Prakriti'. The journey of the divine mind begins from Para Prakriti and also terminates into para prakriti, indicating that our divine mind is born out of Spiritual nature (Yogamaya) and will ultimately dissolve back into the spiritual nature.

For example, in Bhagwat Gita, Lord Krishna says to

Arjuna that my birth (beginning) and death (ending) both are divine or spiritual in nature; therefore, all my actions are also spiritual or divine. But the fools don't know this confidential truth and hence mock my actions by comparing them with the normal materialistic actions that are performed by other ordinary men.

By saying this he meant that whenever he takes incarnation or avatar in our material universe he comes with a divine mind or on a divine vehicle that has both its beginning (birth) and ending (death) in Para Prakriti (spiritual world) itself, unlike the minds of common human beings that are trapped in material universe (Apara Prakriti). Therefore, we should never make the mistake of confusing Lord Krishna with ordinary human beings and compare his actions with those of other men. There is a reason why his actions are called 'Leelas'; it means that the Lord is not performing any actions that are outside of him and happen due to ignorance or illusion (Maya), rather whatever actions that are being performed by the Lord, he is doing it to himself because there is no one else other than him which is a result of right knowledge and complete understanding of Truth, i.e. Yoga-maya. We saw from our human perspective that the Lord was dancing with the gopis, but what we don't realize is that the Lord was always dancing with him and him alone, and there was no Gopi that was other than him. Just like we think our hand is a part of ourselves and take care of it as our own, similarly, Lord Krishna sees every other creature or object of this world as his own part that is not separate from him and therefore naturally takes care of everyone and everything as his own. That's why Lord Krishna is known as the Supreme

Being who has all the divine qualities of a being, namely Atma-Rama, Atma-Ratih, Atma-Kridah, and Atma-Mithun.

The divine vehicle of divine mind is also made up of five absolute layers or sheaths of mind that are also known as 'Five Muktis', which are mentioned in our main scripture, Srimad Bhagvatam, as:

a) Samipya Mukti - Divine Anmay Kosh (Spiritual Body)
b) Sarupya Mukti - Divine Pranmay Kosh (Spiritual Intelligence)
c) Sarshiti Mukti - Divine Mamomay Kosh (Spiritual Intellect)
d) Sayujya Mukti - Divine Vigyanmay kosh (Spiritual Samskara)
e) Salokya Mukti - Divine Anandmay kosh (Spiritual Chitta)

a) Samipya Mukti (Spiritual Body)

According to our scriptures, 'Samipya Mukti' means to be in the association or company of the Lord. We already know that the spiritual world, i.e. Para Prakriti, is made of collective conscience; thus, a spiritual body is not an individual body like our physical body. It is a collective being that always exists as a cult, religion, organization, community, etc., and just like our Anmay kosh (physical body) preserves itself by eating and reproducing, similarly, our divine Anmay kosh (spiritual body) preserves itself by eating spiritual food, i.e. Prasadam, and creating more spiritual beings by teaching spiritual knowledge, i.e. preaching.

Therefore, we can say that 'Samipya Mukti' or spiritual body is something that we can only attain or develop by working on our collective conscience. That is why in all spiritual ashrams it is recommended to participate in the group *sadhnas* or activities to develop connection with our spiritual brothers and sisters during the initial stage of our spiritual journey. Because even if a spiritual aspirant can't do any proper sadhna or perform their rituals correctly, if he or she just remains in the association of spiritual beings or saints and develops a sense of belonging or attachment with them, then they become eligible for getting a spiritual body that is also known as 'Samipya Mukti' or ' Jivan-Mukti'.

For example, whenever Lord Narayana takes incarnation as Lord Rama or Krishna, all the other demigods that are divine beings also have to take birth with the Lord in order to be in his association and also participate in his divine Leelas or past times by serving him through all means. Lord Rama had the support of 'Vanar sena' as his spiritual body, and with Lord Krishna there was the support of 'Pandav sena', i.e. his spiritual body.

(b) Sarupya Mukti (Divine Intelligence):

According to scriptures 'Sarupya Mukti' means to get the form that is as good as Lord Narayana's with four hands holding *sankha* (conch-shell), chakra (discus), gada (club), and padma (lotus flower).

As we discussed earlier that just like our intelligence body deals with the department of ensuring our future safety and survival, similarly, in order for us to attain 'Sarupya Mukti' or 'divine intelligence' we have to ensure the safety and survival of our spiritual body that could be our cults, religious groups, or any other form of spiritual community that we are connected with. Because only then our divine or spiritual intelligence will develop, and then we can attain 'Sarupya Mukti', which means to get the same beautiful divine form that is also eternal and perfect like that of Lord Narayana.

c) Sarshti Mukti (Divine Intellect):

According to the scriptures, 'Sarshti Mukti' means to get the same opulence or powers as Lord Narayana. One becomes as good as the Lord and just as much powerful.

Now as we know that just like our intellect body (Manomay kosh) is mainly concerned with forming and maintaining relationships with others in order to feel complete, similarly, in order for us to develop our divine intellect (Divine manomay kosh) we should form and maintain relationships with the other spiritual bodies and beings. Therefore, we can also say that an ideal or healthy spiritual organisation or institute is the one that allows and gives you the freedom to maintain your relationship with the members of other spiritual organisations or cults as well who may or may not have similar beliefs as ours. That is why, in Sanatan dharma, we are taught the philosophy of 'Vasudhaiva Kutumbakam' which means that the whole earth is like our family, and therefore we must respect everyone's beliefs because only then we will be able to develop our divine intellect and attain 'Sarshti Mukti', which means attaining the same opulence or power as the Lord Narayana.

d) Sayujya Mukti (Divine Samskara):

According to scriptures, 'Sayujya Mukti' means to become one with the effulgence of the Lord. It indicates that just like from the spiritual body of the Lord emerges divine light or radiant effulgence, similarly, those who attain 'Sayujya Mukti' glow as radiantly as the Lord and have a divine aura, i.e. spiritually charged energetic field, around them.

We know that just like our 'Samskara body' (Vigyanmay kosh) tries to keep us consistent, systematic, orderly, and predictable, and basically sticks to certain kind of uniformity in our lives. Similarly, when we go to any spiritual ashram, we are made to follow certain rules or guidelines and perform our sadhna, i.e. spiritual practices, in a systematic manner as prescribed by the spiritual master or Guru because only then can we develop our spiritual Samskara body (Divine Vigyanmay Kosh), also known as 'Sayujya Mukti', which means to have a divine aura or radiantly glowing effulgence like that of Lord Narayana.

e) Salokya Mukti (Divine Chitta):

According to the scriptures, 'Salokya Mukti' means that after leaving the material world one is permanently promoted to the planet where Lord Narayana resides himself, also known as 'Vaikunth-loka', which is in fact our spiritual earth, i.e. the 5th dimension. To attain Salokya Mukti means to get permanent freedom from the temporary cycles of life and death in material realms and shift to eternal spiritual realms where we can have an eternal life. This is why it is also known as 'Moksha', which means ultimate freedom from the painful cycles of transformation, i.e. birth and death.

As we know just like our 'Chitta body' (Anandmay kosh) is known for producing extreme and unconventional desires, similarly, when we choose to opt for extreme measures and go out of the way for the establishment or protection of dharma, i.e. 'Sanatan', only then we can develop our 'Spiritual Chitta body' (Divine Anandmay kosh) and get permanently promoted to the eternal spiritual earth, i.e. Vaikunth-loka, to live eternally with Lord Narayana, which is also known as 'Salokya Mukti' or 'Moksha'. For example, in the war of Mahabharata, we can think of Lord Krishna as playing the role of spiritual chitta (divine anandmay kosh) for Arjuna, who inspired him to kill great warriors like Karna and Bhisma through unconventional ways for the protection and re-establishment of Sanatan dharma.

❖ Diagram of Mind (Apara Prakriti)

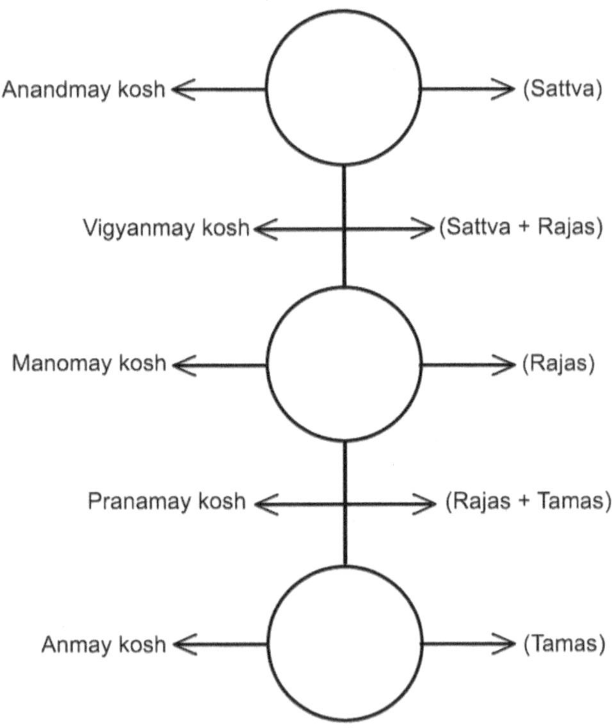

❖ **Diagram of Divine Mind (Para Prakriti):**

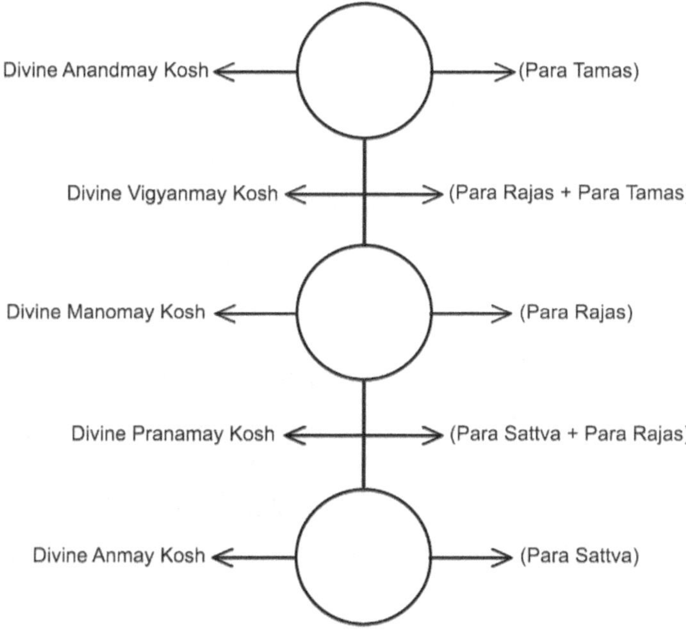

3) Super Mind (Twin Flames)

Super Mind is a vehicle made from the mixture of Pure and Absolute consciousness which travels from Apara Prakriti, i.e. pick-up location, to Para Prakriti, i.e. drop location, and therefore also transforms Purusha, i.e. Shiva, into Param Purusha, i.e. Vishnu.

Super Mind, i.e. Twin-flames, acts as a bridge between Mind (Apara Prakriti) and Divine Mind (Para Prakriti). It is formed by the combination of 6-gunas, both from Para as well as Apara Prakriti. As the 'Jiva-atma' evolves in its spiritual journey the subtle elements (gunas) of Para Prakriti enters into our mind that is made of Apara Prakriti. Then, with the combination of total six gunas both from Para and Apara Prakriti a new 'super-mind' is formed, also known as '*Har- Hari' swaroopam* or Twin flames.

We know that 'mind' is a gadget or vehicle of manifested reality that exists between two polarities of unmanifested reality, that is, the 'beginning' and 'ending'. Similarly, Super-mind projects itself in the manifested reality as two different beings instead of one having common or same source of existence, which is why they are called Twin Flames, meaning one flame divides into two like a nuclear fission. Twin-flames journey begins from Apara Prakriti but always ends in Para Prakriti.

In twin-flame dynamics, one of them is divine feminine (DF), and the other is divine masculine (DM). The DFs have already achieved divinity when it comes to their feminine aspects of the Prakriti as they are naturally very intuitive, sensitive, caring, etc. But their masculine side is still materialistic or Aprakritik; therefore, the DFs need to do inner work in order to transform their masculine side into divinity or Prakritik as well and become a complete divine or spiritual being. When the masculine is transformed into divine masculine, it will compel you to find your soul's purpose and give you the courage to pursue or follow your soul's instincts or calling with determination as these are some of the signs of a healed divine Masculine.

The same goes for DMs as they also have to do their inner work in order to transform their materialistic (Aprakritik) feminine side into divine (Prakritik) feminine, which will compel them to embrace their sensitivity, listen to their intuition, and be more creative as these are some of the signs of a healed divine feminine.

When both the partners have successfully completed their inner work, only then the physical union between DMs and DFs becomes possible as the union of two divine beings; otherwise, separation is inevitable in this journey. Twin-flames do not need to constantly worry about their partners and keep praying for a reunion with them; instead, they should focus on their own inner work, i.e. spiritual growth, if they really wish to help their partners to heal and manifest a physical union with them. Because as we come closer to complete our inner work and transform into a complete divine being, then the nature (Prakriti) itself will force or push your partner or twin soul to heal themselves so that it can bring you two closer for a reunion as a gift or reward for completing your inner work. As it is also the rule of nature (Prakriti) that whatever we create on our inside also has to manifest on our outside, i.e. external reality, sooner or later when the circumstances are favorable it will happen on its own. Therefore, twin-flames do not need to bother about their physical or external reunion with their partners as much as they should be focusing on their inner union or integration of DM and DF within them, as the twin-flame journey is all about transforming ourselves into complete divine beings, and physical union is simply the side-effect or outcome of it.

4) Transcendental Mind
(Transcendental Twin-flames)

A transcendental mind is a vehicle or tool that is made of bliss consciousness through which Adiprakriti, i.e. Super Love, explores or travels into 'Adipurush', i.e. Super Bliss.

It exists beyond Para and Apara Prakriti and has no beginning or ending points whatsoever; like the other three minds, because a 'Lover' has nowhere else to go he or she has already arrived. Therefore, it is also known as 'Transcendental Twin-flames.'

For example, Radhe–Krishna were not like ordinary lovers they were transcendental twin-flames.

❖ The vehicle of transcendental mind is made up of five bliss layers or sheaths of bliss that are also known as five transcendental 'Bhavas' (emotions) or 'Raasas' (mellows) according to Srimad Bhagvatam:

a) Shanta Raas - Transcendental Anmay Kosh (Bliss Body)

b) Dasya Raas - Transcendental Pranmay Kosh (Bliss Intelligence)

c) Sakhya Raas - Transcendental Manomay Kosh (Bliss Intellect)

d) Vatsalya Raas - Transcendental Vigyanmay Kosh (Bliss Samskara)

e) Madhurya Raas - Transcendental Anandmay Kosh (Bliss Chitta)

All the five mellows (Raasas) are different layers of Transcendental mind that function in the following ways:

a) Shanta Raas (Bliss Body)

According to Srimad Bhagvatam, Shanta Bhav or Raas means to feel that I am one with the supreme Lord or Adipurush 'Krsna', who is none other than the Super Bliss himself.

Therefore, in Shanta bhav or raas, a devotee quietly meditates on the super blissful form of the supreme Lord Krsna and becomes ecstatic internally. Transcendental Anmay kosh (Bliss body) tries to preserve itself by eating only 'Krishna Prasadam' and creating more Krsna-conscious beings by preaching about the blissful qualities and glories of the supreme Lord Krsna. Therefore, simply by eating Krsna-prasadam and trying to create more krsna-conscious beings one can surely attain the blissful body, i.e. 'Shanta Bhav or Raas'.

b) Dasya Raas (Bliss Intelligence)

According to Srimad Bhagvatam, Dasya bhav or raas means to feel that I am the servant of the supreme Lord Krsna and always remain in a state of eagerness to serve the supreme Lord. In Dasya bhav or Raas, one constantly tries to engage himself or herself in the service of Lord Krsna and his devotees. For example: Hanuman ji.

Transcendental Pranmay Kosh (Bliss Intelligence) develops when we engage or dedicate our intelligence towards protecting or securing the future of Krishna-conscious devotees. Using their intelligence in the service of the super blissful Lord Krsna, the devotees become ecstatic and thus attain the Dasya Raas or bhav (Bliss Intelligence).

c) Sakhya Raas (Bliss Intellect)

According to Srimad Bhagvatam, Sakhya bhav or raas means to feel that I am the friend of the supreme Lord Krsna and therefore take part in all endeavours of the supreme Lord as his companion or partner to support the Him by all means. In Sakhya bhav or raas, a devotee tries to serve Lord Krsna and his devotees by all possible means to help them accomplish their goals just like a best friend, and in doing so they become ecstatic. For example: Arjuna, Uddhav, etc.

Transcendental Manomay Kosh (Bliss Intellect) develops as a result of forming and maintaining our relationships with the other Krsna-conscious devotees. Therefore, those who engage their intellect to form and maintain relationships with the other devotees of the supreme Lord Krsna and create or support any kind of society, club, or organization for the welfare of Krsna-conscious devotees are the true friends of the supreme Lord Krsna, and therefore, they will attain the 'Sakhya Raas or bhav' (Bliss Intellect).

d) Vatsalya Raas (Bliss Samskara)

According to Sri Bhagvatam, 'Vatsalya bhav or Raas' means to feel that I am the father/mother or provider of the supreme Lord Krsna and have parental instincts towards the supreme Lord and his devotees. In Vatsalya bhav or Raas, a devotee is very affectionate towards Him and his devotees, and therefore, they become ecstatic by taking care of Krsna and providing for his devotees by all means.

Transcendental Vigyanmay Kosh (Bliss Samskara)

develops as a result of following a consistent routine of taking care of the supreme Lord Krsna and his devotees according to the instructions or system prescribed by the vedas or saints. Therefore, those who show complete dedication and leave no stone unturned in taking care of Him and are also affectionate towards his devotees will certainly attain the Vatsalya raas or bhav (Bliss Samskara).

e) Madhurya Raas (Bliss Chitta)

According to Sri Bhagvatam, 'Madhurya bhav or Raas' means to feel that I am the lover of the supreme Lord Krsna and therefore have loving instincts or tendencies towards Him. In Madhurya Raas, a devotee gets filled with the loving and ecstatic emotions simply at the sight of Krsna or even his devotees; especially, when they hear or chant His name, who Himself is Super Bliss personified and actually resides in his names in a subtle form, they become extremely blissful and ecstatic beyond all measures. Those who attain the 'Madhurya Raas' (Bliss Chitta) reside permanently or eternally with the supreme Lord Krsna in his personal and super blissful 'chidanand' kingdom, i.e. Goloka-Vrndavan, as 'Gopi'. ('Gopi' also means gopaniye, i.e. secret or very confidential Tattva.

Transcendental Anandmay Kosh (Bliss chitta) develops as a results of having extreme desire for serving and pleasing the supreme Lord Krsna and going to any possible or even impossible extents for the pleasure of the supreme Lord. Those who think out of the box and find unconventional or irrational ways to break the monotony of desires produced by other four transcendental bhavas or Raasas simply for the pleasure of supreme Lord Krsna will definitely attain the 'Madhurya Raas' (Bliss Chitta) and get permanently promoted to the transcendental and eternally blissful kingdom of the supreme Lord Krsna to live with him in the 'Goloka-Vrndavan' Dham, which is also our ultimate destination or the original home of all souls.

❖ Conclusions

i) 'Parameshwar' (God) travels on the vehicle of mind that is made of pure consciousness within the Apara Prakriti.

ii) 'Param-atma' (Super Soul) travels on the vehicle of super mind that is made from the mixture of pure and absolute consciousness from Apara to Para Prakriti.

iii) 'Param-Brahman' (Super Brahman) travels on the vehicle of divine or spiritual mind that is made of absolute consciousness within the Para Prakriti.

iv) 'Adiprakriti' (Super Love) travels on the vehicle of transcendental or bliss mind that is made of bliss consciousness to explore 'Adipurush' (Super Bliss).

TRANSFIGURATION

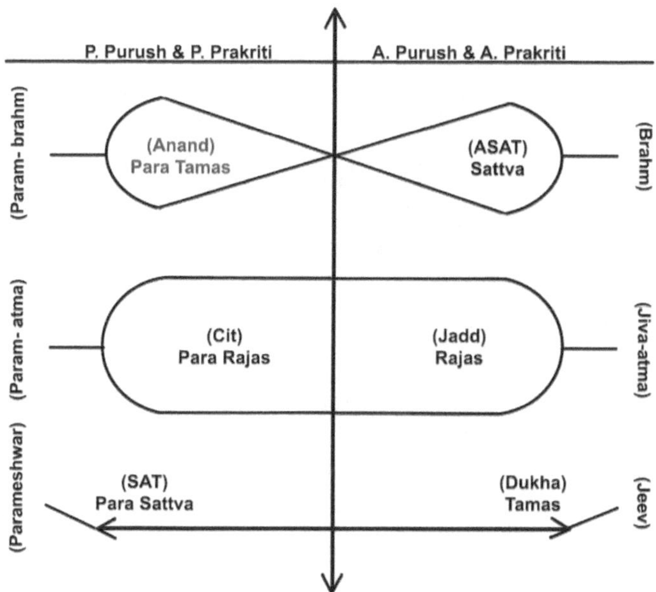

❖ Purush and Prakriti go through seven stages of transformation to finally evolve into Adipurush and Adiprakriti. The stages of evolution are as follows:

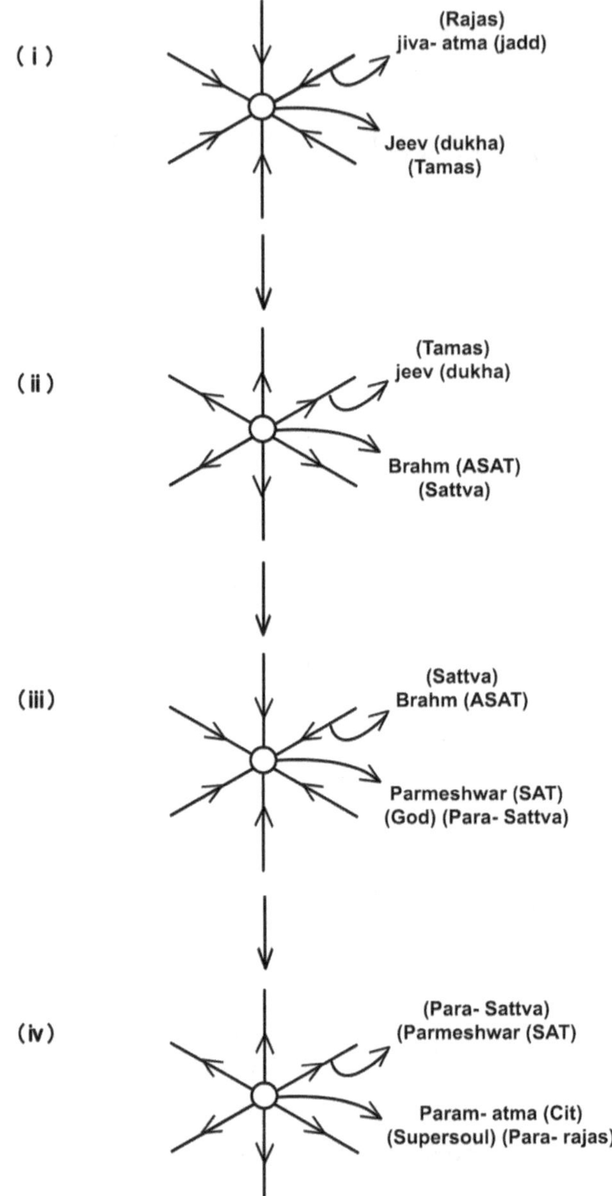
(i)
(Rajas)
jiva- atma (jadd)
Jeev (dukha)
(Tamas)
(ii)
(Tamas)
jeev (dukha)
Brahm (ASAT)
(Sattva)
(iii)
(Sattva)
Brahm (ASAT)
Parmeshwar (SAT)
(God) (Para- Sattva)
(iv)
(Para- Sattva)
(Parmeshwar (SAT)
Param- atma (Cit)
(Supersoul) (Para- rajas)

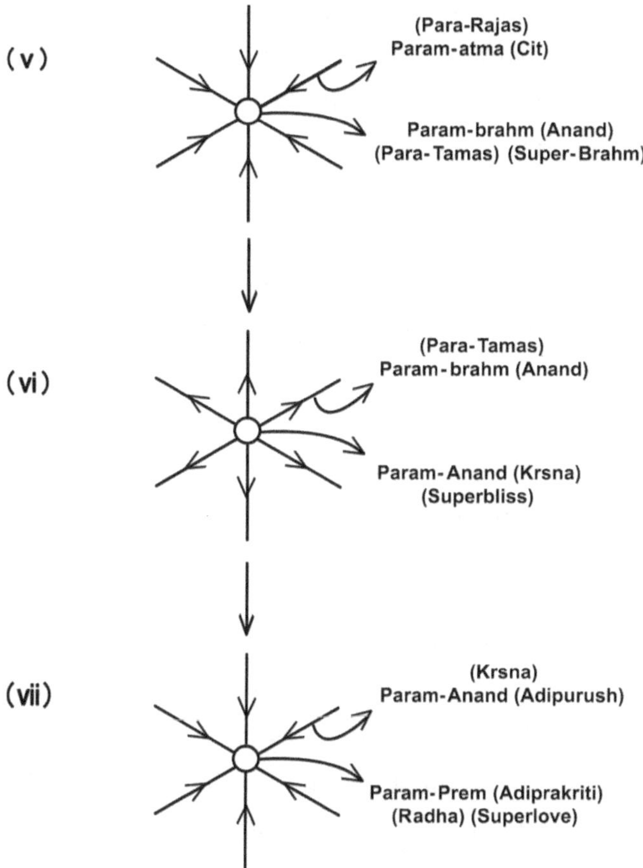

❖ Explanation

(i) At the first stage of evolution 'jiva' is the subject, and 'jiva-atma' is its object. As we know that the object always revolves around its subject, we can say that 'jiva-atma' (jadd/material) revolves around its subject 'jiva' (pain and suffering). Therefore, we can say that all material objects ultimately lead us towards pain and suffering. That's why it is always recommended by the saints or monks those who want to get rid of their pain and suffering should first let go or at least mentally renounce all their desires for or attachments with material objects or material possessions.

(ii) At the second stage of evolution when we let go of our pain and suffering, i.e. jiva, by renouncing all our attachments and desires for material possessions, we get nothingness (ASAT), i.e. 'Brahm', as our subject, and subsequently, our 'jiva-atma', i.e. material consciousness (jadd), transforms into 'jiva', that is, pain and suffering, as our object. Therefore, we can say that all our pain and suffering (jiva) revolves around nothingness (Brahm). That's why most gurus who have realised Brahman (Self) or nothingness suddenly start to see or become aware of all the pain and sufferings that exist within the world of illusion (Maya). Because after Brahman or self-realization, the pain and suffering of others (Jiva) become the objective reality of your life that starts to revolve around its subjective reality, i.e. nothingness (Brahman).

(iii) At the third stage of evolution when we let go of this nothingness (ASAT) or 'Brahman' (Self), we get infinite being or Parameshwar, i.e. SAT, as our subjective reality, and subsequently our objective reality that consists of all the pain and suffering, i.e. 'Jiva', transforms into nothingness (ASAT) and we get 'Brahm' (Self) as our object. Therefore, we can say that nothingness or Brahm (self) revolves around the infinite being (SAT), i.e. 'Parameshwar' or God. That's why those who have realised God or the saints like to spend a lot of time in solitude and enjoy their own company, because for them, now the Self (Brahman) itself has become the object that revolves around its subjective reality, that is, God (SAT).

(iv) At the fourth stage of evolution when we let go of the infinite being or SAT (God), we get infinite consciousness (Cit), i.e. Param-atma (Super Soul), as our subjective reality, and then our objective reality that is nothingness (ASAT) or 'Brahm' (Self) will transform into infinite being (SAT), i.e. God, and we will get 'Parameshwar' or God as our object. Therefore, we can say that the infinite being (SAT), i.e. God, is the object that revolves around its subjective reality, i.e. Param-atma (Super Soul) or infinite consciousness (Cit). Those who have reached at this level of spiritual evolution, to them everyone else is like a God and Goddess because for them now the infinite being, i.e. God, itself has become the object that surrounds its subject, i.e. infinite consciousness or (Super Soul).

(v) At the fifth stage of evolution when we let go of the infinite consciousness (Cit), i.e. Param-atma (Super Soul), we get infinite bliss (Anand), i.e. Param-Brahman (Super Brahman), as our subjective reality, and then also our objective reality, i.e. infinite being (SAT), or Parameshwar (God), transforms into infinite consciousness (Cit), i.e. Super Soul, and we get 'Param-atma' as our object. Therefore, we can say that infinite consciousness (Cit), i.e. Param-atma (Super Soul), revolves around its subjective reality, i.e. infinite bliss (Anand) or Super Brahman (Param-Brahm). Those who have reached at this level of spiritual evolution, to them everything becomes full of consciousness because for them now infinite consciousness, i.e. Super Soul, itself has become the object that revolves only around its subject, i.e. infinite bliss (Super Brahman).

(vi) At the sixth stage of evolution when we let go of the infinite bliss (Anand), i.e. Super Brahman, who is formless, we get Super Bliss (Param-Anand), that is, bliss personified (Krsna), as our subjective reality, and then also our objective reality, i.e. infinite consciousness (Super Soul), transforms into infinite bliss, i.e. (Super Brahman), and we get infinite bliss or Param-Brahm as our object. Therefore, we can say that infinite bliss, i.e. Param-brahm, revolves around its subjective reality, i.e. Super Bliss (Krsna/Adipurush). Those who have reached at this level of spiritual advancement or evolution, to them everything becomes blissful because for them now infinite bliss, i.e. Super Brahman, itself has become the object that revolves only around its subjective reality, i.e. Super Bliss (Krsna).

(vii) At the seventh and last stage of evolution when we even let go of the Super Bliss or bliss personified (Krsna or Adipurush), then finally we get Super Love (Param-Prem) or Adiprakriti, i.e. Radha, as our subjective reality, and then also our objective reality, i.e. infinite or formless bliss (Anand), also known as Param-Brahm (Super Brahman), transforms into bliss personified, i.e. 'Krsna' or Super Bliss (Param-Anand), and we get Adipurush (Krsna) as our object. Therefore, we can say that the Super Bliss or Adipurush himself (Krsna) revolves around its subjective reality of Super Love or Adiprakriti (Radha). This is the final or last stage of our spiritual advancement, after completing which we can experience love in doing everything; moreover, we can see the supreme Lord Krsna everywhere we go because for us now the Super Bliss or Adipurush (Krsna) himself has become our object that simply revolves around its subjective reality, i.e. Super Love or Adiprakriti (Radhe).

❖ Conversion of Apara Prakriti (Pure consciousness) into Para Prakriti (Absolute consciousness):

In Sanatan dharma, there are four yugas that are as follows:

(i) Satyug	=	(Sattva)	
(ii) Tretayug	=	(Sattva + Rajas)	
(iii) Dwaparyug	=	(Rajas + Tamas)	
(iv) Kaliyug	=	(Tamas)	

(i) According to our vedas, 'Satyuga' is specifically designed by the Prakriti in order for us to purify our Sattva-guna, so that we can transcend it; to that end, 'Dhyana-yoga' is recommended as the most ideal method.

For example: Lord Vishnu in 'Satyuga' takes incarnation as 'Parshurama', an ardent devotee and disciple of Lord Shiva who practices 'Dhyan-yoga'. Therefore, we can say that Satyuga, i.e. Sattva predominant, can be purified and transcended with the help of 'dhyan yoga', i.e. the path of meditation.

(ii) According to our vedas, 'Treta-yuga' is specifically designed by the Prakriti in order for us to purify our Sattva + Rajas, so that we can transcend it; to that end, 'Karma-yoga' is recommended as the most ideal method.

For example: Lord Vishnu in 'Treta-yuga' takes incarnation as 'Rama' and demonstrates the most ideal principles and moral grounds on which human beings should build their lives through his selfless actions, i.e. Karma yoga. Therefore, we can say that Treta-yuga, i.e. Sattva + Rajas predominant, can be purified and transcended through the practice of 'Karma-yoga', i.e. the path of performing selfless actions.

(iii) According to our vedas 'Dwapar-yuga' is specifically designed by the Prakriti in order for us to purify our Rajas + Tamas, so that we can transcend it; to that end, 'Gyana-yoga' is recommended as the most ideal method. For example: Lord Vishnu in 'Dwapar-yuga' took incarnation as 'Krsna' and demonstrated the power of knowledge by defeating the entire army of his opponents without using any weapons and also shared with us the divine knowledge of Bhagwat Gita. Therefore, we can say that Dwapar-yuga, i.e. Rajas+Tamas predominant, can be purified and transcended through the practice of 'Gyana-yoga', i.e. the path of knowledge.

(iv) According to our vedas, 'Kali-yuga' is specifically designed by the Prakriti in order for us to purify our Tamas-gun, so that we can transcend it; to that end, 'Bhakti-yoga' is recommended as the most ideal method. For example: Lord Vishnu took incarnation as 'Chaitanya Mahaprabhu' and demonstrated the perfect example of rendering selfless devotional services towards the supreme Lord Krsna and also appointed Acharyas to spread the science of bhakti-yoga for the welfare of all. Therefore, we can say that 'kali-yuga', i.e. Tamas predominant, can be purified and transcended through the practice of 'Bhakti-Yoga', i.e. the path of devotion.

❖ **Now, In Apara Prakriti:**

Anmay kosh	=	Tamas
Pranmay kash	=	Rajas + Tamas
Manomay kosh	=	Rajas
Vigyanmay kosh	=	Sattva + Rajas
Anandmay Kosh	=	Sattva

❖ **In Para Prakriti:**

Divine Anmay Kosh	=	Para Sattva
Divine Pranmay kosh	=	Para Sattva+Para Rajas
Divine Manomay Kosh	=	Para Rajas
Divine Vigyanmay Kosh	=	Para Rajas + Para Tamas
Divine Anandmay Kosh	=	Para Tamas

Therefore:

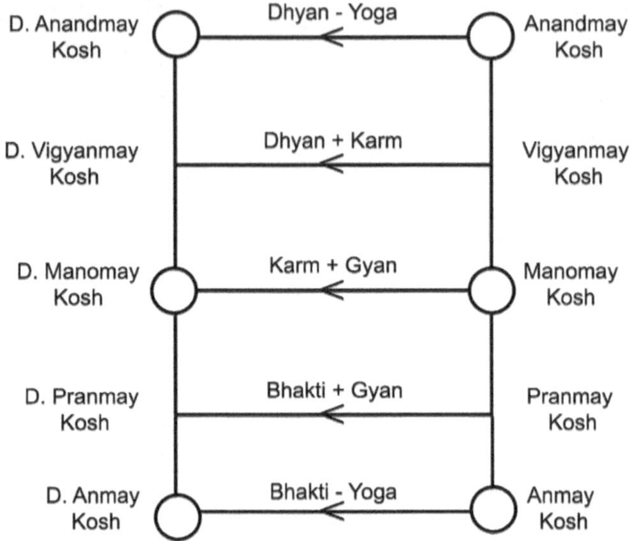

Similarly, Conversion from Para Prakriti (Absolute consciousness) to Adi-Prakriti (Bliss consciousness):

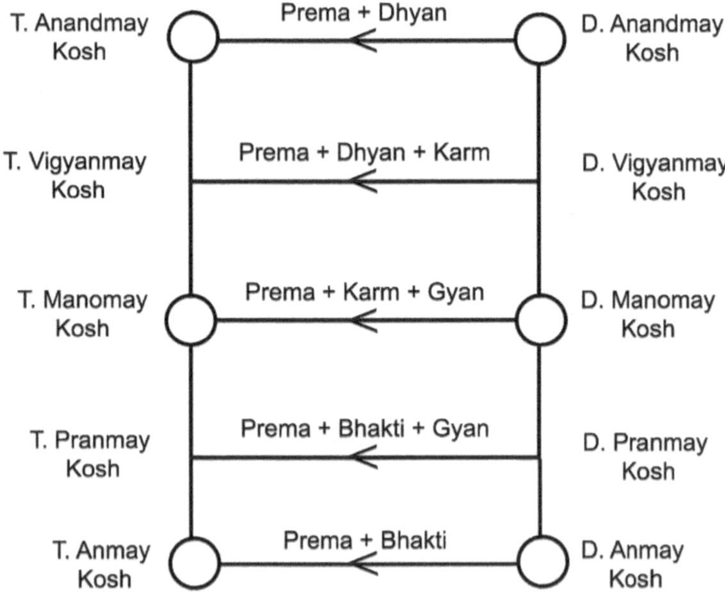

There are mainly five types of yogas:

(i)   Bhakti-Yoga
(ii) Gyan-Yoga
(iii) Karm-Yoga
(iv) Dhyan-Yoga
(v)   Prema-Yoga

❖ The goal of 'bhakti-yoga' is to transcend all our ignorance and desires that are born out of pain and suffering, i.e. Tamas-gun, and establish ourselves in an absolute desireless state, i.e. infinite being (God), which is full of knowledge and absolute purity, also known as 'Para Sattva'. 'Jiva' is the ansh (fragment) that is born out of infinite being (God), and therefore, practising bhakti-yoga allows the individual being, i.e. 'Jiva', to surrender itself completely to the Parameshwar (God) and reunite with the infinite being to become like God again. Therefore, we can say Bhakti-yoga leads to the attainment of our 'Param-Dharma', that is, to reunite with our God or infinite selves, i.e. Parameshwara (infinite being).

❖ The goal of 'Gyan and Karma' yoga is to transcend all our doubts and fears that arise due to our unconsciousness or material (jadd) state of consciousness, i.e. Rajas-gun, and establish ourselves in a state of absolute clarity and power, i.e. infinite consciousness (super soul) by transforming 'Rajas' into 'Para Rajas'. Actually, Gyan-yoga is only the theoretical part that is meant to clear all our doubts and confusions; however, to get rid of all the fears we need to practise it through the art of 'Karma-yoga', which is actually the practical implementation of Gyan-yoga. For example: Just like in our college, we learn theory in classrooms and then also have to perform the practicals or experiments in the lab room to pass the subject examination. Now, our Individual consciousness, i.e. (Jiva-atma) is the ansh (fragment) that is born out of infinite consciousness, i.e. Param-atma, and therefore, practising both Gyan and Karm yoga together allows our individual consciousness (jeev-atma) to surrender itself completely to the infinite consciousness and become one with the 'Param-atma', i.e. Super Soul. Therefore, we can say that 'Gyana and Karma' yoga leads to the attainment of Param-Artha and Param-kama, that is, to reunite our individual consciousness with the super or infinite consciousness, i.e. Param-atma (Super Soul).

❖ The goal of 'dhyan-yoga' is to transcend all our thoughts and attachments that arise out of nothingness (ASAT), that is, 'Sattva gun', and establish ourselves in an absolute thoughtless state, i.e. infinite bliss (Super Brahman), which is full of absolute awareness and detachment, also known as 'Para Tamas'. After detaching from our thoughts we can get access to infinite bliss or unlimited absolute awareness that can make us omnipresent by transforming our 'Sattva' into 'Para-Tamas'. 'Brahman' is the ansh (fragment) that is born out of infinite bliss, i.e. Super Brahman, and therefore practising dhyan-yoga allows individual bliss, i.e. Brahman, to surrender itself completely to the Super Brahman and reunite with the infinite bliss, i.e. Param-Brahman. Therefore, we can say that Dhyan yoga leads to the attainment of Param

Moksha or Kaivalya Moksha, that is, to reunite our individual bliss, i.e. Brahman, with the infinite bliss, i.e. Super Brahman.

❖ The goal of 'Prem-yoga' is to transcend both the gunas of Para as well as Apara Prakriti and establish ourselves into the transcendental state or realms of Adiprakriti, i.e. Super Love. By practising dhyan yoga, we can only get access to infinite formless bliss (Super Brahman) that is scattered everywhere as a consequence of which we have to lose our sense of any identity and attain the state of Nirvikalp Samadhi, i.e. Moksha, which is not our ultimate goal or destination. Therefore, to overcome this consequence, 'Prema-yoga' is practised that allows you to concentrate all the scattered bliss that is in a formless state to give it a form that is also known as Param-anand or Super Bliss (Krsna), who is the personification of the infinite bliss.

Now, on this concentrated form of bliss or Super Bliss (Krsna) awakens a transcendental awareness which is known as 'Prem tattva' or 'Super Love' that doesn't dissolve itself completely in the ocean of infinite bliss and loses its identity permanently (Moksha) but rather floats on it like a lotus flower, thereby transforming absolute consciousness into permanent bliss consciousness that is beyond both Para and Apara prakriti. Therefore, we can also say that 'Prem-tattva', i.e. Super Love concentrates infinite or formless bliss to give it a form just like 'Vivek-tattva', i.e. discretion, can concentrate infinite or scattered awareness at one point. Therefore, we can say the practice of Prema-yoga leads to the attainment of

Param-Prem or Super love (Radha) that is beyond both Para and Apara prakriti.

Theory of Karma (action)

According to the theory of Karma there are three types of Karma or actions:

i) Sanchit Karma (action in sleeping state)
ii) Prarabdh Karma (action in dreaming state)
iii) Kriyaman Karma (action in waking state)

(a) **Sanchit Karm**: All the experiences and memories that we have accumulated as a result of actions that were performed in our innumerable past lives are stored in the form of memory seeds within our causal body and are known as 'Sanchit Karma', i.e. accumulated actions. Therefore, we can say that our Causal body is a storage house that is used by 'Brahman' to keep the records of all our Sanchit Karm or past actions.

(b) **Prarabdh Karm**: All the favourable and unfavourable circumstances that we will encounter within one lifetime manifest themselves as a tree of destiny within our Subtle body and are known as 'Prarabdh Karm', i.e. Destiny. Therefore, we can say that our subtle body contains the blueprint or map of our destiny that is created or designed by the 'Jiva-atma' itself to live or follow its own journey and destination.

(c) **Kriyaman Karm**: All the favourable and unfavourable experiences that we go through as a consequence of our actions within one lifetime manifest or grow themselves as a fruit of fate or fate line according to palmistry within our physical body and are known as 'Kriyaman Karm', i.e. Fate. Therefore, we can say that our physical body is a tool of matter that is used by 'Jiva' to eat and experience or taste the fruits of its own good or bad fate in one lifetime.

❖ **Diagram**

(seed of memories) Sanchit Karm (Brahm)

↓

(Tree of distiny) Prarabdh Karm (jiva-atma)

↓

(Fruit of Fate) Kriyaman Karm (jiva)

❖ **Demonstration:**

According to the diagram, from the seed of memories or thoughts sprouts the tree of our destiny on which grows the good or bad fruits of our own fate that can't be escaped.

It works in the following ways:

1. All our positive and negative thoughts are simply the projections of our good/pleasant and bad/unpleasant seeds of memories or experiences that are stored within our causal bodies by the Brahman, i.e. 'Sanchit Karm'. For example: A thought to eat something arises because of our past experience of eating.

2. Now, the favourable or unfavourable circumstances around which our desires will be experienced or fulfilled is decided by the Jiva-atma according to the Prarabdh Karm or destiny map designed by it. For example: Whether we will get something to eat or not, and if we do get something to eat, then where will we eat it? It can be a five-star hotel or a local restaurant, which is all decided by the Jiva-atma according to our Prarabdh karm, i.e. Destiny.

3. The sweet or bitter fruits of our own positive thoughts (good deeds) and negative thoughts (sinful deeds) will be experienced by 'Jiva' in the form of 'Kriyaman karm', i.e. Fate. For example: The actions or efforts that will be made by the 'Jiva' to eat that food and then go through the experience of good or bad taste of it is all decided by our 'Kriyaman karma', i.e. Fate.

4. Therefore, we can say *why* we do something in our life is inspired or decided by the Brahman through our thoughts, i.e. Sanchit karma; *how* we will do something in our life is inspired or decided by the Jiva-atma according to our destiny, i.e. Prarabdh Karma, and *what* we will do in our life is inspired by the 'Jiva' through our fate, i.e. Kriyaman Karma.

❖ Transformation of Karmas (Actions) into Divine Karmas (Spiritual actions):

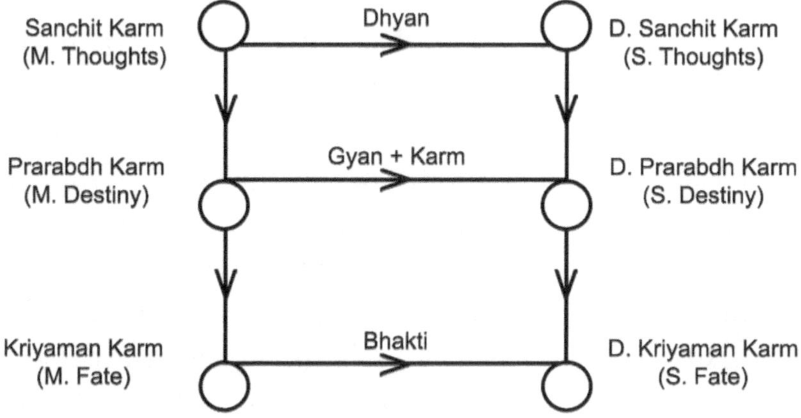

i)   What we call or understand as a 'sin' is nothing but a seed of bad or painful memory that is stored within our causal bodies as 'Sanchit Karma' (accumulated actions). These seeds of unpleasant memories are bound to project themselves as negative thoughts that will eventually lead us to experience our ill fate and commit to sinful activities. Therefore, to eradicate evil or sin from its root, we need to first let go of all the bad or painful memories of the past that we are very tightly holding on to from our causal bodies because they are projecting themselves as negative thoughts that will ultimately ruin our lives by producing the fruits of sinful fate.

The only way to do this is to practise Dhyana-yoga with the help of which we can transform all of our Sanchit Karma (Materialistic Memories) of the past into the absolute fire of Divine Sanchit Karma (Spiritual memories). By replacing all our materialistic memories with the spiritual memories, all of our past memory seeds that were materialistic in nature get burned, and the old causal body is replaced with a new divine causal body that is used by 'Super Brahman' to project spiritual thoughts, which will ultimately grow as the fruits of spiritual fate or spiritual experiences. Hence, we can also say that by the experience of spiritual Samadhi, which is the ultimate goal of dhyan yoga, all the seeds of our accumulated actions, i.e. 'sanchit karm', of the past get burned, and thus all our sins are also destroyed. And we get a brand new divine causal body that only produces holy or spiritual thoughts, thereby always keeping us free or protected from all kinds of sinful activities.

ii) All the good and bad circumstances in which our karmas (action) will be performed and desires will be experienced are stored in our subtle body as Prarabdh karm, i.e. material destiny, by jiva-atma. As a result, we may face favourable or unfavourable situations in our life that are materialistic and therefore full of doubts and fears.

However, with the practice of 'gyan yoga', all our doubts are destroyed; with the help of 'karm yoga', our fears are eradicated, and together they can transform our 'Prarabdh Karm', i.e. Materialistic destiny, into 'Divine Prarabdh Karm', i.e. Spiritual destiny, which is created or designed by Param-atma (Super Soul) with the help of our new divine subtle body.

A spiritual destiny will give us opportunities to go through circumstances that are spiritually favourable so that we can easily accomplish our spiritual goals and become more advance or grow spiritually. Furthermore, we can say that the spiritual destiny that is created or designed by Param-atma (Super Soul) will make us live a fearless life that is full of clarity.

iii) All the good and bad Karmas (actions) that will be performed by the Jiva that will lead to good or bad reactions will be experienced by 'Jiva' with the help of physical body as its 'Kriyaman Karm' or Fate. Depending upon the script of our destiny or Prarabdh Karm, we will have to taste the sweet (pleasure) or bitter (painful) fruits of our own fate. However, with the practice of bhakti-yoga, all these materialistic fruits of pain and pleasure can be turned into spiritual fruits of spiritual pain and spiritual pleasure and thus will also transform our Kriyaman Karm, i.e. fate, into Divine Kriyaman Karm, i.e. spiritual fate, wherein all our Karmas (actions) will be performed and desires will be experienced by Parameshwar (God) himself with the help of our new divine physical body or spiritual body. Therefore, we can say as a result of having the fruits of spiritual fate in our life, we will get inspiration or motivation to perform spiritual Karmas, i.e. divine actions, and as a result, we will go through certain kinds of spiritual experiences in life.

CONCLUSION

Ego, i.e. Jiva, is the ansh or part of Brahman, i.e. Shiva, and it is in its nature to keep on growing by expanding and dissolving itself so that one day it can evolve or develop into Brahm (Shiva), that is, 'infinite space'.

The ego (jiva) is also indestructible like Brahm (Shiva), meaning it can't be destroyed but only transformed which is possible through its dissolution and expansion. The idea of 'ego' as some sort of an evil thing has come from our lack of understanding due to which most people allow themselves or others to suppress it, or let's just say, it becomes very easy for the system to control or restrain us if we start to believe that our 'ego' is something evil that should either be suppressed or gotten rid of. Many people today, whether knowingly or unknowingly, are struggling and fighting with their own ego as they have been taught from childhood that it is evil; thus, they make their lives full of suffering and resistance because they keep fighting the battle that is already lost because there is no way to destroy it.

'Ego' is made of pure energy that can't be destroyed but can only be transformed into its purest form, that is, 'Brahman' (Shiva), and this is exactly what the goal is: to purify our egos and never try to fight with it or destroy it. Something beautiful happens only when we allow our egos to expand themselves infinitely and break free from the boundaries of our limiting belief system. Only then the soul can manifest or integrate itself completely in its absolute form, i.e. 'Satcitanand' or 'Laxmi–Narayan' swaroopam. When this satcitanand soul has manifested or integrated itself completely, a new transcendental awareness of this satcitanand soul also develops or awakens within us, which is said to be 'Chidananda' or 'Radhe–Krsna' swaroopam, our original and blissful form. After attaining this transcendental or 'chidananda' awareness, the soul becomes completely free from the fluids of both pure as well as absolute space and time, which is, after all, an illusion.

Now, to purify our egos (Jiva), we must first understand its significance. Actually, our egos (jivas) are meant to act as a container that is supposed to withhold unlimited amount of spiritual or transcendental bliss and divine love within it. And if we talk about the process of attaining this spiritual bliss and divine love, then it is not like a drop of water that falls into the ocean, but it is rather the opposite, meaning it is like the bursting of clouds where enormous amount of water falls down at one point with all its intensity. Therefore, our container that is our ego (jiva) is required to prepare itself accordingly; otherwise, if our container (ego) is not prepared enough, then it can't withstand the enormous amount of energy that will be generated as an outcome of it and thus could prove to be destructive or even fatal for us. In simple words, if we really want to store an ocean amount of water, then a regular-sized bucket won't be an ideal container.

Therefore, to enable our egos (jivas) to contain unlimited amount of spiritual bliss and divine love, we must first dissolve and expand it infinitely so that it becomes absolutely purified and has the required amount of space within it.

Just like Brahman (Shiva) keeps on dissolving and expanding itself, similarly, its son or fragment, i.e. 'ego' (jiva), also wants to do the same very naturally. Today, all the mental sickness or illness exists within our societies because we all have been told to restrict or restrain our egos, and all our systems are also designed by the devil, i.e. Kali Purush, in such a way that always tries to control or constrict our egos so that we can't grow spiritually, and we accept it because we think, rather, we are fooled into believing that our ego is evil and must be destroyed, which is absolutely wrong and just nonsense. No wonder people who are trapped and became victims of such ego-controlling systems and organizations are becoming sick and losing their mental sanity or health day by day as they are obviously going against their human nature. A healthy ego, i.e. Jiva, dissolves itself first through the practice of 'bhakti yoga', then purifies it by expanding itself with the help of 'Gyan and Karm' yoga, and then finally it becomes infinite to unite with Brahman, i.e. Shiva, by the practice of 'Dhyan yoga'.

If we really knew how valuable our ego (Jiva) is and that one day it will act as a container to hold unlimited amount of spiritual bliss and divine love, then will we ever try or even think of destroying it?

No, absolutely not. We won't, even in our wildest of dreams, ever think of destroying, restraining, or constricting it in any way; we would neither ourselves nor allow anyone else to do the same.

We must allow the ego to follow its natural course, which is as follow:

As the ego (Jiva) dissolves itself, by the practice of 'bhakti-yoga', it is to be purified simultaneously with 'gyan yoga', stretched with 'Karma Yoga', and then finally expanded infinitely with the help of 'dhyan- yoga', thereby making it one with Brahman (Shiva), i.e. 'Pure ego' or 'infinite ego'. Now, only after dissolving itself completely and attaining its purest form, i.e. 'Brahman' (Shiva), the ego (Jiva) is finally ready to contain or withhold unlimited amount of spiritual bliss on which the flower of divine love blossoms like a lotus flower and thus transforms the pure or divine ego into 'transcendental ego.'

The 'ego' (Jiva) is the masculine aspect of the Prakriti; therefore, it has a very natural tendency to be the provider just like all men. Thus, the ego that keeps on providing unconditionally remains in a healthy condition as it is always expanding and purifying itself.

For example: Lord Shiva who controls the masculine force of nature (Prakriti) provides us with all the facilities to sustain our life on earth so that we can grow both materially and spiritually without asking for anything in return from us. Therefore, we can say that providing unconditional service is a very important condition to keep our ego (Jiva) healthy.

Due to lack of spiritual knowledge some people think that when they provide for others they are doing them a favour, but little do they know that it is actually otherwise. The people who are accepting anything from them are doing them a favour by helping them expand their ego (Jiva) so that it remains healthy. The spiritually intelligent men know this secret; therefore, they always remain humble with a heart full of gratitude and also engage themselves in the acts of selfless service. One of the best examples of a healthy ego is Lord Hanuman who always very humbly worships Lord Rama and always remains eager to serve the Lord unconditionally.

All the sins or impurities of a man are washed away by the supreme Lord immediately if only one engages himself in the acts of selfless service. The one who knows this secret about the ego (jiva) and performs all his actions or service with a selfless intent, such a yogi even while acting is not at all acting and is known as Niskama 'Karma yogi'. Such a yogi becomes very dear to the supreme Lord, so much that they don't have to ask or beg for anything anymore in front of any God or Goddess. Because for such a selfless Karm Yogi, the supreme Lord himself becomes servant and looks for opportunities to serve that selfless yogi. One more thing we should keep in our mind that the Supreme Lord is 'omnipotent', which means whatever we think of as merely an imagination or impossible can immediately be manifested or turned into reality by the Lord simply at his will. Therefore, for the Selfless Karm yogis nothing is impossible as even the supreme Lord sometimes changes his own will just to fulfill the wish of such a selfless yogi.

For example: 'Bhism Pitamah', a character of Mahabharata, was a selfless Karm yogi at the time of Dwapar yuga, for whom the supreme Lord Krishna had to change his own will by breaking the promise of being neutral and not using any kind of weapon in the war, only because Bhisma was determined to compel the Lord to pick up his weapons. So the Lord gives up and breaks his promise for him. This leela was simply done by Lord Krsna to prove the exalted position of selfless Karm yogis for whom the supreme Lord is ready to forsake his own promises and change his own will if that's what it will take to make him happy.

❖ In Prakriti, as we already know, everything exists in duality, meaning there will always be a subject and its objects. Therefore, to become free from anything in this Prakriti, the most important rule is to always focus on its subject.

For example:

(i) To become free from our 'body', focus on its subject, i.e. 'Mind'.

(ii) To become free from the 'mind', focus on its subject, that is, 'Brahman' (Atman/Self).

(iii) To become free from 'brahm' focus on its subject that is 'Parameshwar' (God).

(iv) To become free from 'God', focus on its subject, i.e. 'Param-Atma' (Super Soul).

(v) To become free from 'Param-Atma' (Super Soul), focus on its subject i.e. 'Param-Brahm' (Super Brahman).

(vi) To become free from 'Param-Brahm', focus on its subject, that is, 'Param-Anand' or Super Bliss (Krsna).

(vii) And finally, to become free even from 'Param Anand' or 'Super Bliss' (Krsna), focus on its subject, i.e. 'Param-Prem' or 'Super Love' (Radhe).

❖ Now what we call as brahman or atman (soul) is nothing but simply a thoughtless thought or state. In dhyana yoga, a yogi sitting for several hours chasing the thoughts to its origin in the process of meditation comes to the realization or becomes aware of this thoughtless thought (Nothingness/Brahm), out of which all other thoughts arise; thereafter, that yogi contemplating on the thoughtless thought or nothingness (Brahm) remains in the state of 'Savikalp Samadhi' and should be known as 'Self-Realized' saint.

❖ Similarly, Parameshwar (God) is also nothing but just an 'eternal thought' that is born out of 'eternal thoughtless thought', also known as 'Param-Brahm' (Super Brahman). In Bhakti yoga, when a yogi chases after eternal thoughts (Gods) to its origin, he finally comes to the realization or becomes aware of the eternal thoughtless thought (Super Brahman); thereafter, by contemplating upon it the yogi attains an eternally blissful state, also known as 'Nirvikalp Samadhi' or 'Moksha', and such yogis are known as 'God-Realized' saints.

And what we call as Super Bliss or Param Anand (Krsna) is nothing but a form of eternal love that is born out of formless eternal love or super love (Radhe). In Prema yoga, when a yogi chases after eternal love with form, i.e. 'Super Bliss' (Krsna), to its origin, at last he comes to the ultimate realization and finally becomes aware of the formless eternal love, also known as 'super love' (Radha); thereafter, by contemplating upon it he attains an eternally ecstatic state that is indescribable in nature, also known as 'Transcendental or Bhava' Samadhi, and such yogis are known as 'Love-Realized' saints.

Q.) How do we love our original creator or the Supreme Lord Krsna?

- To love our creator or the supreme Lord, the first thing we need to do is to understand his nature and find out all about his qualities because only then it is possible to attain the love of our creator or supreme Lord Krsna.

   The creator (supreme God) is by nature infinite, and therefore all his creations are also infinite, be it anything from universe, galaxy, humans, planets to stars; everything that we can see in this creation is countless or infinite.

   Therefore, when we pray for love from God, he can only bless us with his infinite love or nothing. Many innocent people turn against or give up on God because they are not aware of this condition for the love of god; that's why they simply think out of ignorance that many tragic or painful events happened in their life and the Lord never showed any mercy on them. However, this is not true because these people do not understand that the supreme Lord Krsna is not meant for showing us just a little bit of mercy or grace because anything that is little or finite doesn't exist in his dictionary. The supreme God or creator is only meant for showering us with infinite love and bestowing unlimited grace upon us. Therefore, only those who have developed or created infinite space within their hearts can truly attain or withhold the infinite love and unlimited grace of the supreme Lord; otherwise, for those who think that they can store all the water of ocean in their regular-sized bucket are simply fooling themselves by expecting the unexpected to happen.

Q.) What are the conditions of the supreme Lord Krsna for loving us?

• The lord doesn't require any reason and has no conditions for loving us at all because his love is absolutely unconditional, as even our scriptures declare him to be 'causelessly merciful'. That's why most people who are hoping to impress God by doing any kind of rituals, *tapasya,* or *sadhna* and claim that they have attained the love of supreme Lord (Krsna) by doing any *japas* or *vratas* are simply demeaning the supreme Lord and also defying his nature or quality of being causelessly merciful. Therefore, any saint or guru who are claiming to bestow divine love upon their disciples are committing serious offence against the supreme Lord (Krsna) as no man, guru, or saint can ever become the owner of divine love; it solely belongs to and is owned by the supreme Lord (Krsna) himself. We may become the possessor of divine love by the ultimate grace and mercy of the supreme Lord, but we can never own it. Therefore, all gurus or saints and their prescribed sadhnas can only help us in purifying our souls, and then the divine love will enter into our lives on its own without any reason or conditions by the ultimate grace and mercy of the supreme Lord Krsna alone. Thus, those who want to attain the divine love of supreme Lord Krsna don't need to beg for it in front of any sadhu or saint because it is simply useless. The only way to attain his divine love is to directly approach the supreme Lord Krsna himself, as the lord is omnipresent, and surrender to him alone because only the supreme Lord Krsna himself has the right to grant us with the ultimate boon of divine or super love, i.e. Gopi-tattva. A guru or saint is only allowed to grant us with all the muktis or moksha, but the gift of divine love is only meant to be given by the supreme Lord Krsna himself.

The only thing that the supreme Lord expects from us in exchange for his divine love is that we must develop or have infinite space within our hearts; otherwise, where will we store all his infinite love? Therefore, to create infinite space within our hearts we are required to develop infinite acceptance for everything that is created by the supreme Lord. The depths of our hearts are simply reflected by the quality of our knowledge, never the quantity, for the supreme being and his creations.

For example: Lord Shiva is considered the epitome of acceptance, who has accepted the supreme being and his creations most perfectly and completely; even the things that are considered poisonous and heinous by us are accepted by Lord Shiva. That's why he is known as the perfect devotee of the supreme Lord.

Now, those who wish to attain the divine love of God should always remember that on this path, Super Love (Radha) alone is the guru, and everyone else is its disciple; thus, all are equal in the eyes of the supreme Goddess (Radha). This is exactly why on the path of love, i.e. Prema Marg, Guru–disciple relationship can't exist. For this path, only friendship is recommended as the most ideal, as no feelings of inferiority are involved in this particular relationship; there is only equality, which is the most important condition for the development or nurture of Super Love. Therefore, a true lover of the supreme Lord Krsna should always consider everyone and everything in this creation as their friend.

A true lover of the supreme Lord neither worships nor hates anyone or anything in this existence because both these emotions create attachment with the illusion. When we worship something, we will go to heaven, and if we hate something, then the doors of hell shall open for us. Both these places exist only within the realms of illusion, i.e. Maya. Therefore, it is forbidden for all the yogis who aspire to attain the divine love of the supreme Lord. On the path of love, the Supreme Goddess (Radha) alone is the subject of our friendship or worship, and one must become neutral towards everything else in this existence.

Precautions

Always remember that on any spiritual path or sadhna, vairagya (detachment) is the primary condition because doing any type of spiritual sadhna without detachment is like filling a pot with a hole in it. No matter how many litres of water one may pour in such a faulty pot, eventually all the water is going to drip out of it. Therefore, all spiritual aspirants must try to cultivate the quality of 'vairagya' (absolute detachment) within them before doing any spiritual sadhna to get the best results and maximum output from their spiritual efforts.

Warning

We must understand that getting born into this material world and living our lives carelessly on our own terms is not called life. Actually, what we call or understand as life is an ongoing process of giving birth to our eternally blissful body that contains within it the divine love of the supreme Lord Krsna.

Just like pregnancy is a process through which all women have to go before giving birth to a baby, and during this period of pregnancy she has to be extra cautious simply because the baby in her belly is very fragile and can be easily harmed or killed, similarly, getting a human body or human birth means that we have been impregnated with the seeds of divine love by the almighty, which happens only by chance and to the very fortunate souls. And that's why, after getting a human birth, one must be extra cautious with his or her actions as the seeds of divine love are also very fragile at first, and grave mistakes like committing serious crimes or indulging in sinful activities may prove fatal for its growth, i.e. Divine Love.

A human birth is once-in-a-lifetime opportunity for us to attain the divine love of the supreme God Krsna, which is even desired by the demigods (Devas) that live in the heaven, and they are all willing or wishing to get an opportunity to take birth as human beings and attain this divine love of Krsna. Therefore, those who are not careful and always indulge themselves in unwanted tendencies will eventually lose their seed of divine love from their hearts, or in other words, the almighty will snatch it from them and thus convert them into impotent 'demons' who are incapable of offering or accepting any kind of love.

These impotent demons (Asuras) are doomed to exist in Hell (Apara Prakriti) for all of eternity, and therefore, their only job is to create all kinds of distractions or obstacles for us to destroy the seed of divine love from our hearts to make us impotent too of love and trap us into hell for all eternity just like them. Therefore, one must be very careful and should accept this human birth as a blessing from the almighty god and therefore should always focus on its ultimate purpose, that is, to nurture and attain divine love for supreme Lord Krsna within our hearts. If we deviate from this path or goal for whatever reasons, then we will have to face its severe consequences by spending the rest of our eternity in either 'heaven' or 'hell', both of which are only an illusion (Maya) that is devoid of true love and is not our ultimate destination (Golok-Vrndavan). Therefore, let's just say that those who live their life sincerely and successfully attain the divine love of god and become eternally immortal and infinitely blissful because for them the ultimate reality, i.e. the kingdom of supreme God, is way more beautiful than they can ever imagine. But those who fail to do so, for them even the idea of any ultimate truth or reality is quiet frightening, and therefore they don't want to accept it or simply choose to live under ignorance as for them it is the only way to be blissful.

Final Advice and Instruction

The Apara Prakriti or pure consciousness in which we exist right now is full of pain and suffering, but it is not at all meaningless. There is a hidden purpose behind all our pain and suffering. In our existence, i.e. Apara Prakriti, everyone is suffering but for different and various reasons. However, the Prakriti provides us with free will to choose the reason behind our suffering, as whatever the cause we choose for our suffering is understood by the Prakriti to be very valuable for us, and therefore, it will be used by the creator to define our 'subjective reality', following which our 'objective reality' also adjusts or shapes itself accordingly.

For example:

(i) Someone in their previous life who suffered a lot due to physical illness and didn't get the right treatment for his ailments will develop natural compassion for other people who are suffering due to physical illness. Thus, in their next life they may most likely choose to become doctors and try to cure people from physical diseases.

(ii) Someone who chose to suffer a lot in the search of God by doing spiritual sadhnas or practices in their previous life will naturally develop compassion for other souls who are struggling on this path, and it would become unbearable for such a person to see them in pain because he also has gone through that same suffering due to which now a fire of compassion burns within his heart for every spiritual aspirant, which will automatically compel or inspire him to become a saint or Guru.

Therefore, we can say that by choosing the reason of our suffering we have the power to shape our own destiny. Thus, we can become whatever we want in this Prakriti. The more valuable the reason that we choose for our suffering in this Prakriti, the more valuable of a person our destiny will make us. And trust me when I say this, there is nothing more valuable in this entire existence than Super Love, i.e. Radhe; therefore, those who suffer or strive for the attainment of this supreme Prema Tattva (Radhe) are the wisest and most fortunate because, one day, destiny will most definitely make them even more valuable than the Gods in heaven, and they will attain the residency of the most valuable place which is beyond all creation (good) and destruction (bad) and is actually our original home where the supreme personality of Godhead (Krsna) resides himself within his personal abode, i.e. Goloka-Vrndavan.

Today, most of the systems and organizations that exist within our world are designed to make us suffer and strive for only materialistic pleasures or things that are of no value or meaning, and therefore, it will ultimately trap us in the hellish or lower dimensions, i.e. Apara Prakriti, in which we are living right now.

But the time has come where all these corrupt systems and structures that are forcing us to strive for trivial things in life and only pursue materialistic pleasures are not going to sustain any longer because it is not at all favourable for living in the higher spiritual planes of existence. Right now we are going through a period of radical change and transformation where our planet earth is making a massive shift by taking us into higher spiritual dimensions of existence, which can also be understood as a paradigm shift that is currently taking place on our planet earth. Therefore, if we really want to catch up with these new upgrades or changes and survive in the future to experience a brand new reality of our new earth, which is especially designed for spiritually evolved beings, then we must prepare our people to adapt and transform themselves spiritually, that is, in accordance with the higher frequencies and vibrations of our new earth to ensure the survival of mankind.

The time has come where we must take a stand against our old corrupt materialistic systems and structures that are no longer serving our Prakriti and are only keeping us stuck in lower vibrations of existence. The mankind is on the verge of making a massive evolutionary jump or quantum shift of all time that is not only biological but also happening within our innermost spiritual core or level. That is why there is an urgent need for this generation to ignite the fire of a 'spiritual revolution' at this point in time where it has become absolutely essential for our survival and existence on the new earth. The old materialistic systems and structures will start crumbling and falling down once we all learn to embrace our spirit (Soul) and learn to unleash the power of its creativity and knowledge in order to replace our old corrupt materialistic systems with a new spiritual flavour or theme that is favorable for our spiritual evolution and thus create a spiritual environment, i.e. Para Prakriti, for our overall spiritual wellbeing.